Memories of a Curious Bear
Book 2

Bernie Meadows

A family memoir for those who wish to improve their understanding of the English way of life and English social history, while learning English as a foreign/second language

The book was set in *Adobe InDesign CS3* by John P. Frisby.

Published by *Mospeate Publishing*, Mospeate House, Sheffield S10 3RG, UK

ISBN 978-0-9564949-4-8 (pbk)

Foreign Language Study: English as a Second Language; History: Social History; Biography and Autobiography: Childhood Memoir

To my wife, Pat, and all the other powerful Homertonians

Acknowledgements

I am indebted to a number of people for help, advice and encouragement, and especially to John Frisby, my editor and book designer, for his steadfast and unstinting support. Without his help the book would probably never have come to completion.
Thank you, John.

My thanks also to Hilary Page for her proof reading and for publishing the book via her company Mospeate Publishing.

Thank you, Pat, John and Alex for your long-lasting and loving support.

Published by *Mospeate Publishing*

Contents

Preface

It is difficult to write good, standard English because of the way that its spelling, punctuation and grammar are interlinked. Consider the following pairs of sentences:

1(a) "Alexander the Great" needs to be read again.
1(b) "Alexander! The grate needs to be red again!"

2(a) Alexander understood their knot. Here was a problem!
2(b) Alexander understood. "They're not here," was a problem.

These acoustically similar but semantically different sentences give a hint of why English can be very difficult to write correctly.

I began to write my autobiography after I had visited He Shan Middle School in Fu Jian, China, in 2006 and 2007. Over a period of two years I sent 72 anecdotes to the Chinese teachers at the rate of two memories every fortnight, responding to their request for material that would help teach English but at the same time inform students about the English way of life

It was my old friend, John Frisby, who suggested that I should self-publish my work, using Amazon as our selling agent, and we published our first book in 2012, with the help of Dr. Hilary Page.

Book 2 continues my story. Once again it combines social history with a way to study the English language. The book should be of interest to four groups of people:

(1) Young people who are interested in everyday life in England at the end of the British Empire, over seventy years ago,

(2) Older people who may wish to be reminded of their own childhood,

(3) Students of English as a second or foreign language who wish to learn more about English culture, and

(4) Native English speakers who like puzzles and wish to remind themselves of the principles of English punctuation. (Page vii gives advice on how to do this.)

I have made use of Fowler (1926): H.W. Fowler, A Dictionary of Modern English Usage, Oxford at the Clarendon Press, and

Fowler (2004): R.W. Burchfield, Fowler's Modern English Usage, Oxford University Press.

How to Use and Enjoy This Book

My purpose has been to provide a book which is informative, entertaining, and helpful for those who are studying English.

(1) **Punctuation Exercises**

At the end of the book are some unpunctuated passages which have been taken from my texts. They provide the reader with the opportunity to consider how to punctuate such stories. English punctuation is far more complex than Chinese, and there may sometimes be more than one way to punctuate a phrase.

The reader may also produce his or her own unpunctuated passage from one of my texts and then punctuate it a few days later.

(2) **Dictation**

It can be very helpful if a teacher or student chooses a short passage from one of the *Memories* and reads it aloud for others to write down. About eight or ten lines would be sufficient. First of all, the complete passage should be read aloud. The teacher should then read a group of three to five words, pause for a few seconds, and then read the phrase again. After giving the students time to write down the phrase, the teacher continues the process until the end of the text. He or she then reads the whole passage aloud for the last time.

(3) Notes

Asterisks in the text refer to *Notes* at the end of the book. These give general information and some comments about the grammar.

(4) Copy and Change

Students may copy out a passage but change it in some way. For example:

(a) change the 1st person into the 2nd or 3rd person: 'I' changes to 'you', 'he' or 'she'.

(b) change the past into the present: e.g. 'was' becomes 'is'.

(c) change adjectives and adverbs into their opposites: e.g. 'old' becomes 'new' or 'young'; 'quickly' becomes 'slowly'.

Further activities

Some teachers and students may like to use photos, maps, charts and pictures in the book in order to create new opportunities for speaking English.

(1) A teacher or student asks a question about an illustration starting with one of the words: Who, What, Where, When and Why? Another student tries to provide a suitable answer.

(2) One person makes a statement about an illustration. Someone else has to say whether or not it is *True* or *False*.

(3) The teacher, or one of the students, thinks about something in a picture and the others have to find out what it is by asking questions. It helps if the word is written on a piece of paper before the questions begin.

(4) Someone looks at an illustration and begins to describe it. The rest of the group see who can be the quickest to find the page number for that illustration. A skilful speaker will make correct statements which are so general that it may take some time for the correct answer to be found!

(5) A student may like to take the ideas presented in a memory and use them as a starting-point for giving his or her own ideas, or story. This could be written down as an essay and also presented as a speech.

(6) There may be one or two mistakes which have been left in my text and artwork. An observant reader might like to give fellow students the page number of the error and then see how long it takes them to find the mistake.

Family Trees

m. = married, dots join the couple;
solid lines show children

Chart 1 The Meadows Family

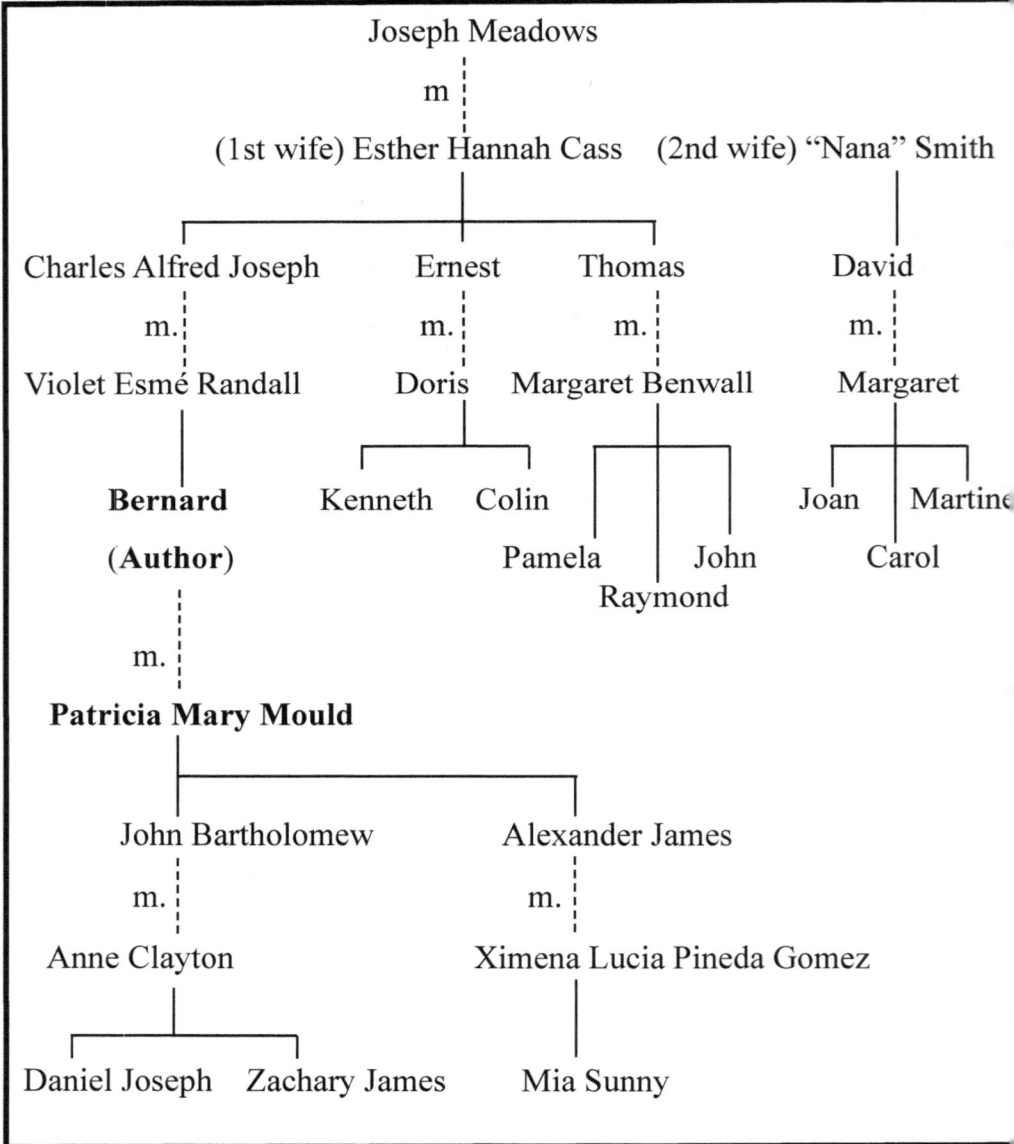

Joseph Meadows

m

(1st wife) Esther Hannah Cass   (2nd wife) "Nana" Smith

Charles Alfred Joseph   Ernest   Thomas   David

m.   m.   m.   m.

Violet Esmé Randall   Doris   Margaret Benwall   Margaret

Bernard   Kenneth   Colin   Joan   Martine

(Author)   Pamela   John   Carol

Raymond

m.

Patricia Mary Mould

John Bartholomew   Alexander James

m.   m.

Anne Clayton   Ximena Lucia Pineda Gomez

Daniel Joseph   Zachary James   Mia Sunny

x

Chart 2 The Randall Family

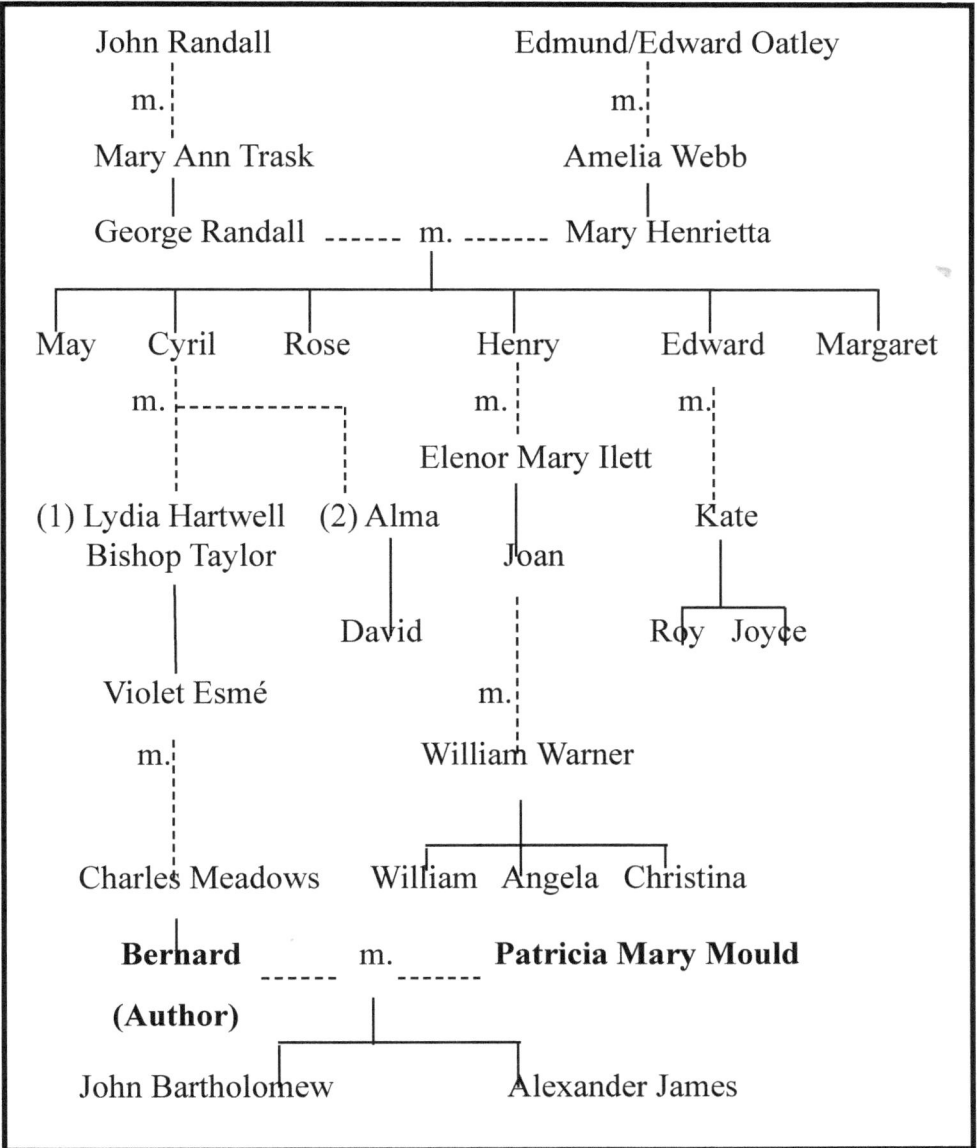

John Randall

m.

Mary Ann Trask

George Randall ------ m. ------- Mary Henrietta

Edmund/Edward Oatley

m.

Amelia Webb

May   Cyril   Rose   Henry   Edward   Margaret

m.

(1) Lydia Hartwell   (2) Alma
    Bishop Taylor

Elenor Mary Ilett

m.   m.

Kate

David

Joan

Roy   Joyce

Violet Esmé

m.

Charles Meadows   William Angela Christina

m.

William Warner

Bernard   m.   **Patricia Mary Mould**

(Author)

John Bartholomew   Alexander James

Note The full name of the author is *Bernard Randall Meadows*. It is quite common practice in the UK for middle names to be a family surname. [*Editor.*]

Chapter 1

1945 WHETSTONE

List of Memories

1. St. James's School
2. The Great North Road
3. My Report Book
4. Elocution Lessons (1)
5. Elocution Lessons (2)
6. Playground Games (1)
7. Playground Games (2)
8. Playground Games (3)
9. Playground Games (4)
10. Beyond the Playground

11. Indoor Games (1)
12. Indoor Games (2)
13. Indoor Games (3)
14. Indoor Games (4)
15. All Saints Church
16. Christianity and Sunday school
17. Scouting and the Cubs
18. Some Activities with the Cubs
19. Guns…
20. …and More Guns!

1 Map of Whetstone and North Finchley

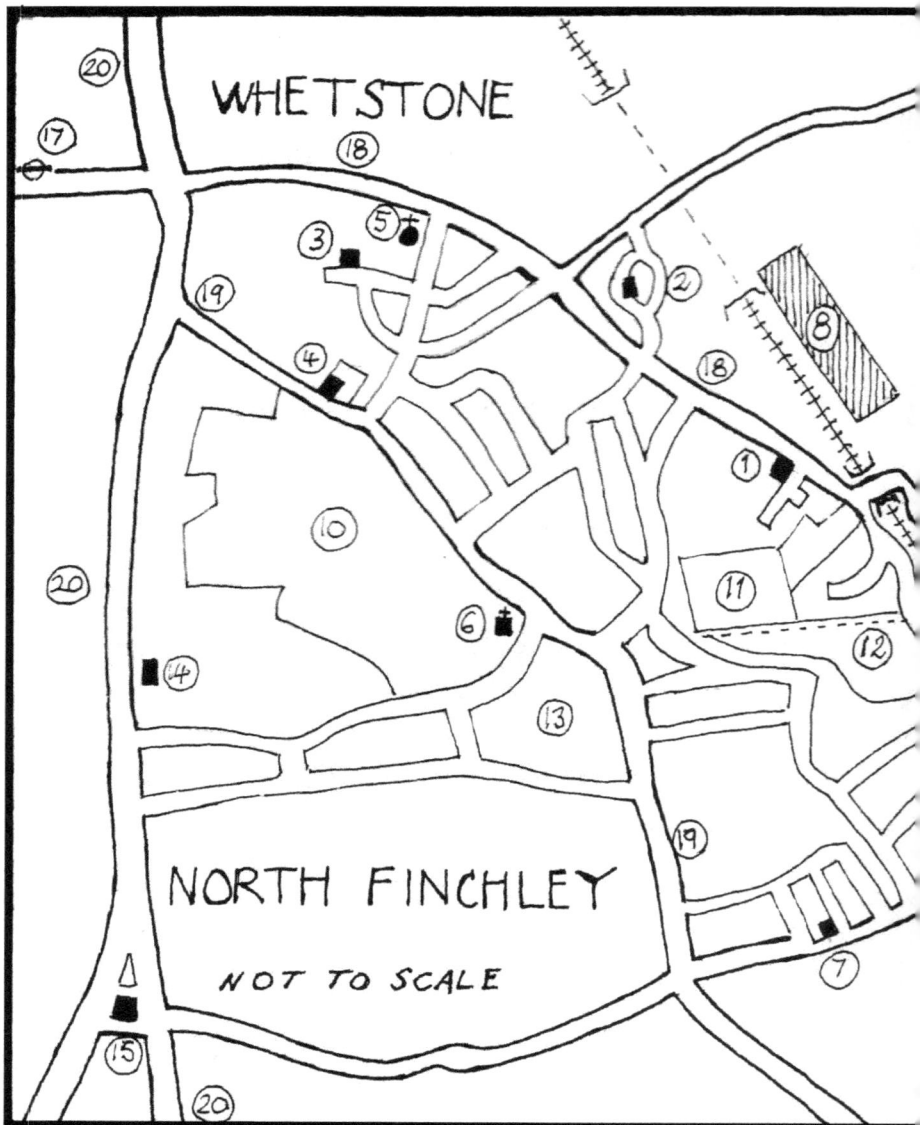

WHETSTONE

NORTH FINCHLEY

NOT TO SCALE

Roads and places which were important to me when I lived in Whetstone 1945-1948:

1. My home

2. John Stanley Browne's home

3. Frederick Murphy's home

4. St. James's School

5. All Saints Church

6. St. James's Church

7. Friern Barnet Library

8. Standard's (Standard Telephone and Cable)

9. Lander's Corner (monumental mason)

10. North Middlesex Golf Course

11 . Bethune Golf Course

12. Bethune Park

13. Friary Park

14. Odeon Cinema

15. Gaumont Cinema

16. Recreation Ground

17. Totteridge and Whetstone Underground Station

18. Oakleigh Road

19. Friern Barnet Lane

20. The Great North Road: A1000

1 St. James's School

In 1945 I had been away from home for nine months. I was aged eight and a half⁺. My evacuation to Somerset in order to escape the bombs and rockets of World War II had given me a cultural shock. I had moved from a suburban flat in North London, with its gas, electricity and plumbing, and I had gone to live in Dinder – a village which was so small that it didn't even have a pub.

My great-aunt's cottage had been built in 1589. It had no gas, electricity or plumbing. There was a privy at the far end of the garden, and drinking water came from a pump close to the back door. A paraffin lamp provided us with light, and a stove was used for cooking and heating. I had grown used to this way of life from August 1944, and when my mother came to fetch me home in May 1945, I had mixed feelings. I was sorry to leave Dinder and yet I was also happy to be going home. I also looked forward to attending the St James's Primary School from which I had been absent for two terms.

My mother took me to see the school on Tuesday 15th May and I started there as a pupil on Monday 28th May 1945.

The school consisted of two buildings, one of which appeared to have been built in the twentieth century. The other building had flint stone walls and was presumably built at some time in the first half of the nineteenth century, because the school first opened its doors to pupils in 1853.

I spent the summer term and the whole of the next year in classrooms situated in the old building. I have seen a photo of one of the rooms which is much the way that I remember it: the ceiling was high and angled upwards like the ceiling of an Anglo-Saxon hall.

My last two years were spent in a classroom in the new building.

[⁺Editor's Note: The author was born on 17th November 1936.]

2 St. James's School
The 19th century building and its porch are on the left, and the modern 20th century building is on the right. In front of them was the playground.

Our teacher was called Miss Leroy, but we called her "Marly," which was short for Ma Leroy. It was in this class that I came to know the two boys who were to become my oldest friends – John Stanley Browne and Frederick Murphy.

John Browne (see *Postscript*) had been at Oakleigh Infants before being evacuated to Leeds with his mother, brother, and two sisters, but I don't remember him at the infant school. Fred had attended a different infant school before coming to St. James's. I usually sat next to Fred or John, or in their vicinity. I remember that on more than one occasion our conversation caused us to break into a fit of uncontrollable giggling. I was certainly sent to stand outside the door several times and I seem to remember that we had to be split up from time to time.

On the whole my friends and I were very good, because we were able to cope with the work, which we enjoyed. However, I remember that I was once caned on my hand by the Headmaster though I can't remember what I had done wrong.

2 The Great North Road

St James's School was situated in Friern Barnet Lane (**1**, page 2; labels 4 and 19), It was about a quarter of a mile (about four hundred metres) south-east of the Great North Road. In the Middle Ages* Friern Barnet Lane was part of the route out of London but it came by way of Muswell Hill.

Apart from having to traverse the obstacles of Muswell Hill and two other hills on its way to Whetstone, the Great North Road was poorly maintained and often muddy and full of ruts. In the eighteenth century the Bishop of London gave up some of his land so that a new road could run across Finchley Common (not shown on the map in **1** as it no longer exists as an area of open public-ownership land). This was much better because the new Great North Road now ran along a ridge and the journey therefore became much easier from London until the road reached the steep hill at Barnet.

One disadvantage, however, was that highwaymen began to frequent Finchley Common. Many travellers were robbed of their money and valuables (**3**), and some of the highwaymen were not as gallant and romantic as the stories would have us believe. Some bloody deeds took place in the Finchley and Whetstone areas.

It is for this reason that travellers began to stop at Chipping* Barnet (now known as High Barnet) for the night, before travelling on to London the next morning. When I was a boy there were still several public houses in Barnet which had been coaching inns in the eighteenth and nineteenth centuries.

We no longer have highwaymen in the Finchley area, or indeed anywhere in the UK, and many pubs have closed down in Barnet and elsewhere in England since the Second World War.

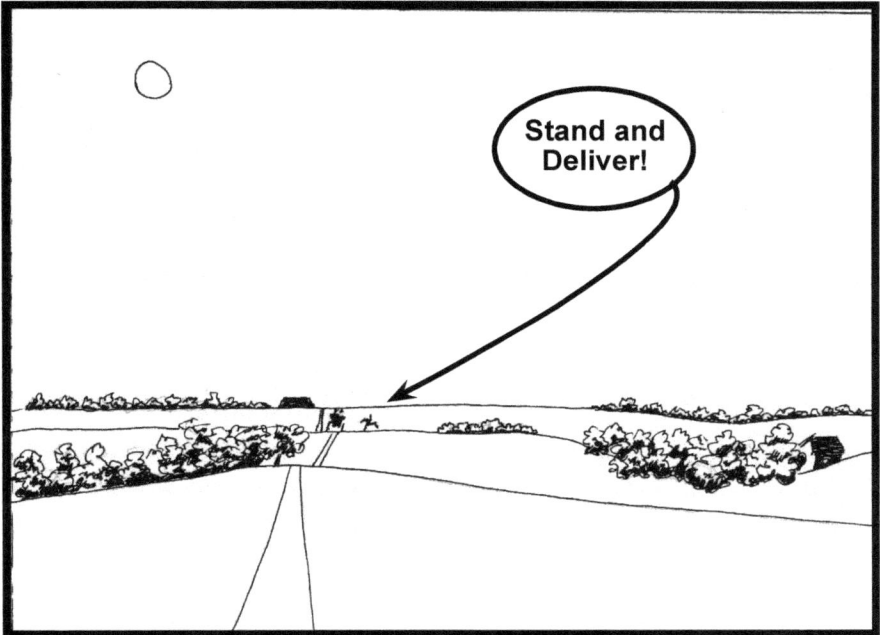

3 A Highwayman on Finchley Common

"Stand and Deliver!" is what highwaymen are said to have shouted when they stopped a coach. What had to be delivered were the valuables of the passengers.

3 *My Report Book*

Mr. T. E. Greaves was the Headmaster of St. James's School during the time that I was there. I still have my report book which indicates that I was happy in the school and made good progress, but not all the comments by teachers were complimentary.

For example, in July 1945 my first teacher wrote that I was too talkative. Although I scored 81% overall, and my English marks came to 91%, my Arithmetic score was a disappointing 57%.

A year later, in July 1946, my second teacher wrote about my mental arithmetic and ability to solve mathematical problems: "Good. Still much too slow – must speed up next year." However, with regard to my Handwriting, Dictation, Composition and English in general, he wrote: "Good. Has excellent knowledge of words & their meanings."

Fortunately, I managed to improve my maths and my position in class was usually near the top. I came 5th in the class in my first term (Class 4) and 4th in class (Class 3).

4 St. James's School
Here is another view of the 19th century building, where it faces
Friern Barnet Lane. We played Five Stones in the porch on the right.

I then moved from the rather gloomy old building into the much brighter and more attractive modern block. For some reason or other I missed Class 2 and spent two years in Class 1, where I dropped down to 9th out of 48 in July 1947.

I eventually managed to reach 6th out of 45 in the December of that year, and finally achieved the satisfaction of coming 4th out of 45 in July 1948.

My progress was partly due to the encouragement of my parents and teachers, but the Headmaster also did his best to encourage me. In July 1945 he wrote: "Bernard has settled down very well. He is a most promising boy who should do well." In February 1946 he wrote: "One of the most intelligent boys in the school, Bernard should have been top boy. Make your mind up lad!"

After two more similar reports he wrote in July 1948: "So ends a very happy and successful four years here & I am extremely sorry to lose him. The future is bright with hope as he goes to Woodhouse with my sincere wish for success and happiness there in even greater measure. Best of luck lad. TEG." [*Editor's Note*: TEG are the initials of Mr. T. E. Greaves.]

However, many years later, Fred Murphy reminded me that the Headmaster had stressed his desire that his pupils should get to local grammar schools and that they should avoid going to Holly Park, the local Secondary Modern School.* I had forgotten that Mr. Greaves was contemptuous of boys who were not academic.

His attitude certainly helped me, but it can't have helped those boys who were not keen on studying for its own sake. Similarly, our regular tests in class may have been elitist, but they probably helped me to make better progress than I would otherwise have done.

4 Elocution Lessons (1)

From the very beginning of my time at St. James's School the Headmaster, Mr. Greaves, exerted an influence on my educational progress even though he didn't teach me directly. On the 29th May 1945 he wrote a letter to my mother as follows:

Dear Mrs. Meadows,

May I say* at this early stage how pleased I am to have Bernard. He is settling down to his work, & already I have found him to possess more than average intelligence. I have every confidence that he will do well.

He is such a well-spoken little chap that the idea occurs to me that you may care to have him taught elocution privately. I mention this because a young friend of mine who is training shortly for speech therapy work is commencing a small class in elocution at which she is very good.

She is in the 5th form at the Woodhouse School....Her fee is 15/6 (£0-77) for 12 lessons & she lives in Gresham Avenue, just by Bethune Recreation Ground.

If you are interested I would be pleased to give more details. Bernard deserves the best we can do for him,

Sincerely,

T.E.Greaves, Headmaster

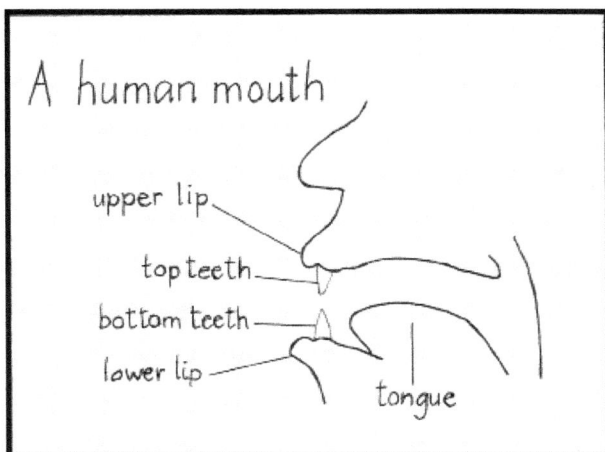

A human mouth

upper lip
top teeth
bottom teeth
lower lip
tongue

5 A Human Mouth
Some specialists say that the various parts of our
mouth are performing a dance when we speak.

My parents were worried about my way of speaking because I tended to rush what I was saying; perhaps this was because I had a lot of ideas which I wanted to express as quickly as possible. They were also worried that I might pick up a Cockney* accent from some of the boys around me, which was not thought desirable for a child of lower middle-class parents! They were therefore happy to accept Mr. Greaves' suggestion.

During my life I have noticed that many people in England don't bother to speak very clearly. The Germans say that we are "mundfaul", i.e. mouth-lazy, and I'm inclined to agree with them. Public announcers, e.g. those who address the people waiting at a railway station or drivers who speak to us on the underground trains, are often incomprehensible. I'm also guilty of poor speech at times, but my experience with Cynthia Stanley provided me with an awareness of how to articulate words clearly. I like to think that this knowledge has helped me to communicate better with other people and to study various foreign languages more effectively. I wish that some managers would take more trouble to train public announcers to speak more clearly.

5 Elocution Lessons (2)

On Wednesday 13th June 1945 I attended my first elocution lesson with Miss Stanley and continued to benefit from her teaching for the next three years. At the time I didn't think that they were very important, but I've come to realise that these lessons were indeed valuable.

Firstly*, I became more aware of the sounds of Standard English and the importance of articulating words clearly. Even though I still have a tendency to mispronounce words when I'm keen to put forward a strongly-held point of view, I try to make myself slow down and express myself clearly.

Secondly, I learned to appreciate the value of reciting poetry aloud and the possible beauty of the spoken word while at the same time becoming more critical of what I was reading. I didn't like most of the poetry which we read because I found it too childish, and since those days poetry has always been low on my list of interests. Nevertheless, I have written several poems of my own, but only when I felt a sudden urge to do so. I have also come across a number of poems which I liked very much, but only because each one had some special relevance to me and my personality. At least two poems in my later life have made me cry, presumably because they have tapped into some deep semantic level which affects my emotions, but generally speaking poetry doesn't appeal to me very much.

Thirdly, for some strange reason we practised mime! Perhaps some of Miss Stanley's pupils hoped to become actors or actresses. The ability to act without speaking and to indicate meaning by gestures has been useful to me throughout my life and especially as a special-needs teacher and as someone involved with foreign languages.

I later realised that there are two kinds of mime: 'symbolic' – rather like the sign language used for people who are deaf and/or dumb, and 'realistic' – in which the actor moves his body in order to suggest what is happening.

For example, when pretending to hold a pistol, some people make their hand into the shape of a gun (**6**). They point their index finger, or their index and middle fingers, while bending their thumb over the other fingers. I prefer to shape my hand as though I were holding the gun (**7**) by bending my index finger as though I were squeezing the trigger and curling my middle, ring and little fingers as though holding the handle. Similarly, some people make the shape of a telephone receiver with their index and little finger, whereas I prefer to pretend to hold a phone – with my fingers curled around an invisible receiver.

6 A Symbolic Pistol
This is the way that some people like to represent firing a handgun.

7 Holding a Pistol
Here is someone miming how to hold a handgun in a 'realistic' way.

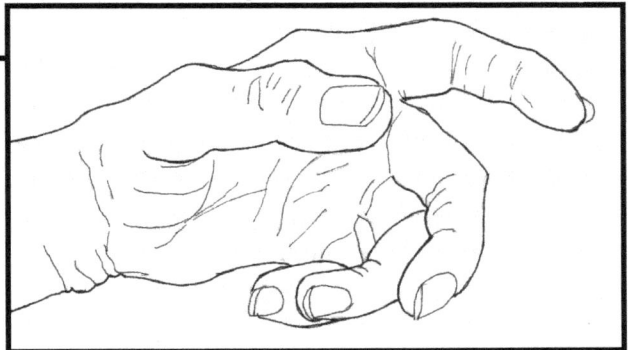

6 Playground Games (1)

When I later became a teacher I realised that children don't come to school in order to receive an education; they come to school in order to meet their friends and have fun. Sometimes they're able to have some fun in the classroom, but their main pleasure comes from making their own entertainments with their friends, such as playing games during break-time and lunch-time. It's one way in which we learn how to get on with other people.

I can remember several games which I enjoyed immensely during my playtimes at St. James's, two of which were chasing games. In order to commence such a game we needed to choose someone to be the chaser and we usually used the little rhyme "*One Potato.*"

One boy, perhaps the one who had suggested the game, would recite: "*One potato, two potato, three potato, four; five potato, six potato, seven potato, more.*"

The other boys would stand in a circle with their two fists held in front of them at waist level and the reciter would chant the rhyme as he walked around the circle. While chanting the words "*One potato*" he would strike the first fist and so continue counting around the circle in the same way until he came to the eighth fist which he would knock down. He would then say, "*You're out!*"

After this he would continue reciting his way around the circle knocking down every eighth fist until he reached the last one. When he knocked down the very last fist he would say to the boy: "*You're 'He'*" or "*You're 'It.'*" This boy would then start to chase the other boys as quickly as he could.

Incidentally, I wasn't sure if my memory was correct as to the pronunciation of this chant. We should have said: "*two potatoes, three potatoes...*" etc., but I remember that it was easier to drop the 's/z' sound at the end of each word.

In his book *The Story of English in 100 Words* (2012) the eminent linguist, David Crystal, quotes the same chant on page 104. I found this very reassuring when I read his comments.

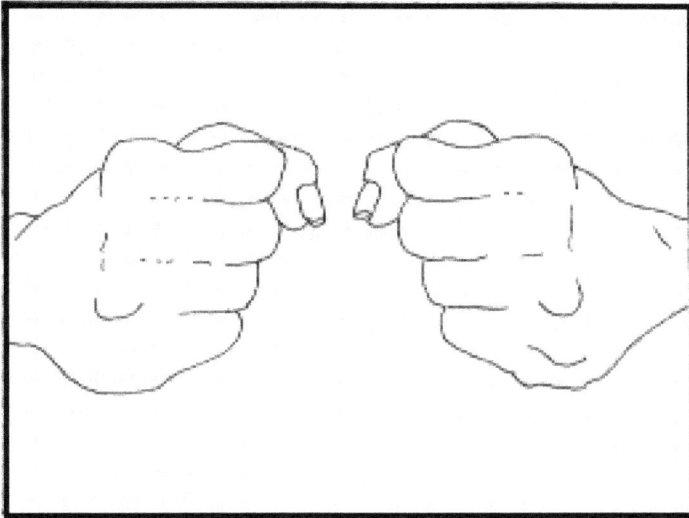

8 Two Fists
This is how a boy would hold up his two fists for 'counting out.'

7 Playground Games (2)

My favourite playground game was a ball game, the name of which is one of the few words which I don't know how to spell in English – partly because of the vagaries of English spelling and partly because I can't find it in my copy of Collins English Dictionary. It was called *Kingy* (pronounced king-ee). In some parts of London the same game is called *He-ball*, because it involves one boy chasing the others. The word 'tag' can mean a chasing game and I believe that I've also seen the word Tag-ball.

One boy starts bouncing a ball – usually a tennis ball – and chases the others around the playground. He keeps bouncing the ball, but when he sees an opportunity he throws it at one of the other boys so that it hits him on his body below his neck, above his knees and anywhere on his upper arms above his elbows.

Any boy who is being chased can strike the ball at any time with his fist. If the boy who is 'It' misses his target, someone or other will probably hit the ball as far away as possible.

The first boy to be struck successfully by the ball joins the chaser. Now they stop bouncing the ball and must pass it backwards and forwards to each other. While one boy has the ball the other one can run freely and will therefore try to get close to a possible target.

Towards the end of the game, when only a few targets are left, it's possible for most of the boys to surround someone. He will then squat down and protect himself by hiding behind his shins and forearms! The others throw the ball backwards and forwards over his head, trying to outwit him, while he spins around to face the ever changing threat.

This activity must have helped our ability to throw things accurately. In any case, I loved this game because it gave me plenty of exercise while I was able to use my brain to think ahead as to where the next attack was likely to come from!

9 The Game of *Kingy*
Here is one of the boys defending himself near the end of the game.

8 *Playground Games (3)*

Once or twice I joined in a game which was derived from books we had read and films we had seen: it involved such elements as finding secret passages, and required a great deal of telling each other what we were going to do. *"We go to the end of the corridor and find that there's no way to get out, but then I find a secret panel. I go through into the room but a net drops on me and you come and rescue me..."* Needless to say, I don't think that we played this very often as it was a rather slow and cumbersome game.

Far superior was the game of *Off-Ground Touch.* A small area of the playground was chosen and the players agreed that various items provided places of refuge. They were usually slightly above ground level, but there were also items which could be touched, such as a drainpipe. After one boy had been chosen to be "It" the rest would scatter to places of refuge.

From time to time a boy would run to another refuge. If it was occupied, the boy already there had to vacate it. Any boy who was touched by the chaser then became the new "It."

The game was more exciting if there were more boys than places of refuge. Ideally it should follow the formula "$r = p\text{-}2$", where p is the number of players and r is the number of places "off ground," as long as* there are at least five players. It can be just as demanding on legs, abdomen and the respiratory system as tennis, squash and badminton.

This is a wonderful game and I only wish that I could have played it every day of my life; then I wouldn't have had to worry about becoming too fat.

I'm surprised that no-one has set up special facilities to play *Off Ground Touch* in the way that people have provided tennis and squash courts. A small hall or 'court' of that kind could be used for 'Off-ground touch,' as well as for playing *Kingy*. Players waiting to join a game and other members of the public could sit in a viewing area, which could be part of a café. I can't help asking myself whether a twenty-first century entrepreneur will take up my idea and make a lot of money out of it! "Could such games ever become part of the Olympics?"

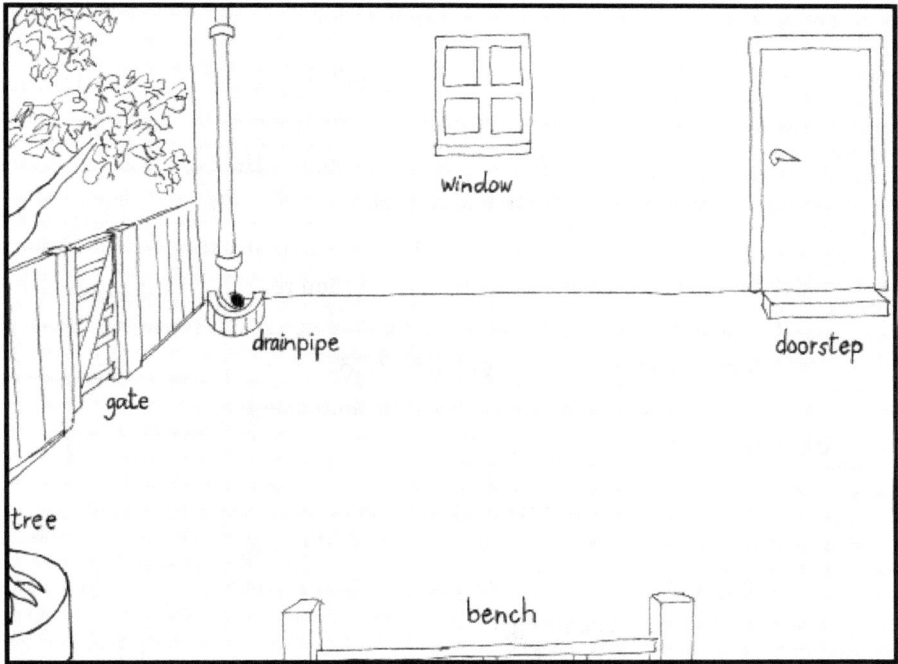

10 *Off-ground Touch*
This view of a playground shows some of the items which could be used as safe places 'off ground.'

9 Playground Games (4)

My school friends and I didn't always spend our break times running madly around the playground. There were many times in the last year or so of primary school when, on fine days, I would sit with a few others in the school porch playing *Five Stones*. This game is also called *Knucklebones* and was known in Ancient Greece, where the players used bones taken from sheep. Instead of using pebbles we bought our sets of 'stones' from toyshops. Each stone was a cube with sides which were about half an inch (one centimetre) long.

Like most good games it was simple and yet complex! The first player would take the five stones and throw them down on to the floor of the porch or the asphalt surface of the playground. He then took one stone and threw it into the air. He had to pick up one of the other stones with the same hand and then catch the first stone as it came down. Having placed one stone down on the ground he then repeated the process with each of the other three stones. The next stage was to throw up a single stone but pick up two stones together. And so it went on. Each stage of the game became increasingly difficult and more complicated.

It was similar to the game of snooker, because the next player didn't have a chance to play until the first player had made a mistake. In that respect I suppose that it encouraged us to sit quietly and patiently – a good thing for young boys to learn!

11 Five Stones
Here is a hand throwing up a stone (left), picking up three others (middle; stones hidden from view) and then having caught the first one while holding the other three stones (right).

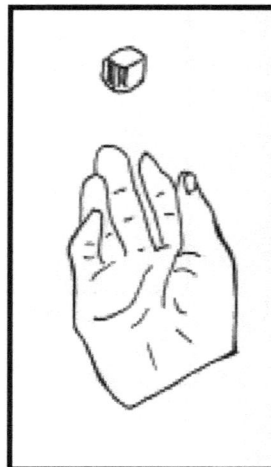

It may also have increased our dexterity because it gave us practice at improving our hand-eye coordination.

In September 2014 my old friend and editor, John Frisby, reminded me of the game of *Chain-he*. I had forgotten this, although I seem to remember playing it once or twice. One boy chased the others until he caught one of them and then they held hands while chasing the rest of the group. As they gradually caught other boys by managing to touch them the chain became longer and more unwieldy, but it also became a longer and more effective net.

In the late 20th century I learned of the Indian game, *Kabaddi*. In this game two teams take it in turns to send a single player to invade their opponents' side of the court while the members of the other team hold hands and try to trap the invader. I wonder where and when, and by whom, this idea was first invented. Perhaps it was first played long ago by early hunters.

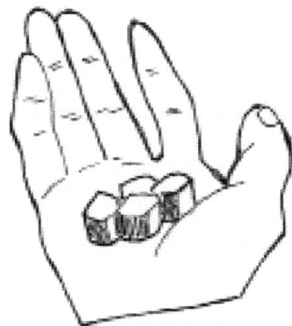

10 Beyond the Playground

Opposite the school on the other side of Friern Barnet Lane was the North Middlesex Golf Club. This was a private club and the grounds extended for about half a mile (800 metres) along the road and were about a quarter of a mile (400 metres) wide. The clubhouse was about two or three hundred yards downhill of the school and a belt of woodland extended from it northwards as far as the school and perhaps as much as a hundred yards beyond. This woodland, which ran alongside the road, was only about twenty yards (15 metres) wide, but it contained a great many trees and a considerable number of bushes, shrubs and general undergrowth.

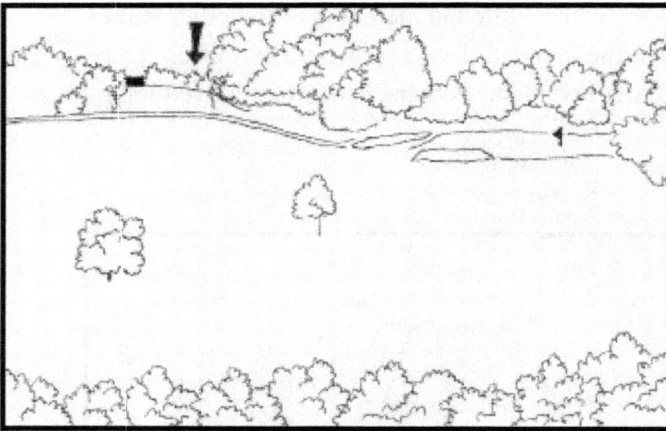

12 North Middlesex Golf Club
This scene is viewed from two directions: the right-hand side is seen from the southeast corner, but the left-hand side is from the east. The black arrow shows where we used to play.

From our point of view this woodland was an urban wilderness. During my last year at St. James's a boy called Bowman (who I think first suggested the idea) and I and one or two others, got into the habit of creeping out of school at playtime; we would cross the road, find a hole in the fence and then play games in this 'forest.' We made a little 'house' inside one particular bush which was so well camouflaged that it was hidden from view until we came very close to it.

13 The Golf Club 'Jungle'
This picture gives an impression of the kind of woodland in which we played. You can see the golf course between the trees.

As far as I can remember the fence enclosing the golf club grounds in that area was a wooden one and so helped to shield us from the view of passers-by. Part of the fun was to keep ourselves out of sight of the golfers on the greens and the fairways, but the woodland was so dense that we were never discovered.

I hate to think what would have happened to us if we had been discovered. I also feel sorry to think of what might have happened to the headmaster and his staff if it had become known that several boys had left school during school time. It was a different age then. Nowadays they would be pilloried* by the press for having paid too little attention to the requirements of 'Health and Safety.'

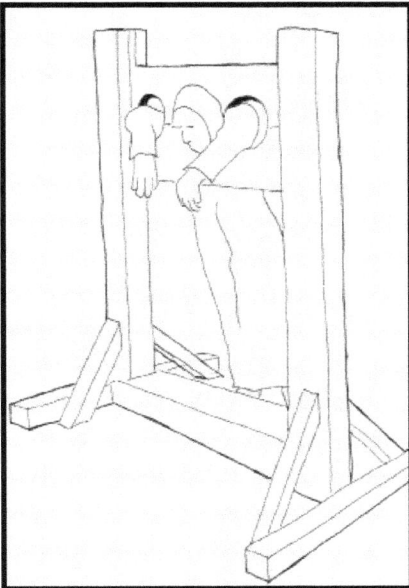

14 A Medieval Pillory
This was a form of punishment in the middle ages.

11 Indoor Games (1)

I've already mentioned that I used to play *Halma* and *Draughts* with my mother, but I didn't really like them very much – their range of moves was too limited for my taste. There were a couple of other board games which, although also quite simple, were more appealing to me, perhaps because they included an element of chance.

Ludo, from the Latin meaning "*I play*," was a game for two, three or four players. The square-shaped board had a 'home' at each corner and there were four coloured counters for each home. The colour of each set of counters matched the colour of their home. There were squares forming a track which ran around the board and past the homes to a central target.

Each player chose a colour. One by one the players took it in turn to throw a die and then move one of his or her counters along the track for the same number of squares as were shown on the die. The first one to return all four counters to the centre was the winner.

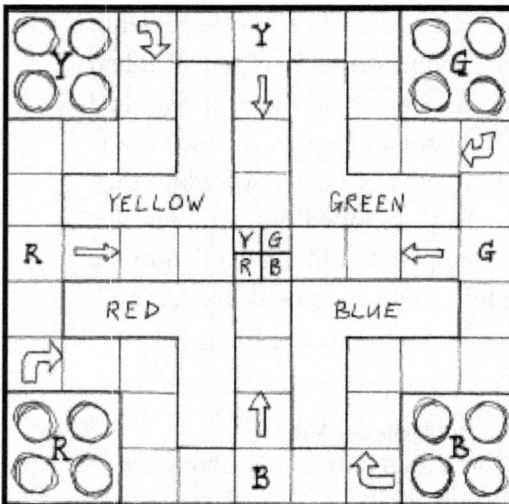

15 The Game of *Ludo*
An example of a Ludo board.

Another popular board game, with counters and dice, was *Snakes and Ladders*. This was more picturesque than *Ludo* because, although the board usually consisted of numbered squares, there were several snakes and ladders portrayed as stretching between pairs of numbers.

Each player in turn shook the die in its box and threw it onto the table. That player's counter was then moved along the track, which ran backwards and forwards across the board from the bottom left-hand corner. A player who came to a ladder was able to move the counter to the top of the ladder, which could be several levels higher than its base. Landing on a snake square would bring a player downwards. Naturally, the first player to reach the final square at the top of the board was the winner.

In some games there was a text which told a story: a lucky event at the bottom of a ladder would take you upwards; a misfortune at the tail of a snake would bring you downwards to its head. I suppose that I understood from an early age that chance was part of our lives, and I've also come to realise that I've been extremely fortunate in my life.

16 The Game of Snakes and Ladders

12 *Indoor Games (2)*

While I was still an infant I was given a set of large, green *dominoes* with pictures of animals on them. I kept them with my toy bricks and used them to construct 'buildings' for me to bomb. I used this set to play dominoes with my mother once or twice but later learned to play with a standard set.

The standard set of dominoes consists of twenty-eight small, black, rectangular blocks, which are sometimes called 'tiles,' on which are marked the numbers one to six. These numbers are not in Arabic or Roman numerals* but are shown by white spots.

Each domino shows two numbers – one on each half of the tile. Some of the dominoes include a blank on one half and there is also a double-blank. Six of the dominoes have the same number on each half.

In most games the dominoes are placed end to end on the table, so that the number, or blank, at one end of the new domino matches the end number of the domino which is already on the table. This makes a line of dominoes. Those with a double number or the double-blank are placed at right angles across the line.

To begin the game the dominoes are shuffled face down on the table. The players then take an agreed number of dominoes and stand them up in front of them so that each player can see only his or her own dominoes. They take it in turns to lay a domino down next to one or other end of the 'line.'

A domino set is rather like a pack of cards in so far that it can be used to play a variety of games. I believe that there are many more games which can be played with cards, but dominoes have the advantage that they can last a lifetime, whereas a pack of cards soon deteriorates.

When I was young, dominoes was* a very popular game in pubs and years ago I played it several times with friends while out drinking in the evening. It can be a very enjoyable game, but I've never studied it seriously.

17 The Game of *Dominoes*
This photo shows a game of dominoes in progress.

13 Indoor Games (3)

When I returned to Whetstone, having played Whist in Somerset, it was natural for me to continue playing cards. My only partner was my mother and it's not possible to play proper whist with only two players. She therefore showed me how to play *German Whist* which is suitable for two players.

The rules are the same as for normal Whist but only half the cards are dealt out. The others are left as a pack on the table and the top card

18 *German Whist –* Stage One
Here are the 'hands' of two players. The top card in the pack on the right is the Ace of trumps!

is turned over. This card indicates which is to be the trump suit during that game. The players each put down a card in order to win this top card. The one who loses the trick picks up the next card for him- or herself and then turns over the new top card of the pack. This card is then taken by the winner of the next trick, and so the game proceeds. The number of tricks won or lost is not important; what matters is the value of each card which is taken from the pack.

When the last card of the pack has been taken the second stage of the game commences. Each player still has thirteen cards and it is now that the players keep count of the number of tricks which are won or lost. The player who wins the greater number of tricks is declared the

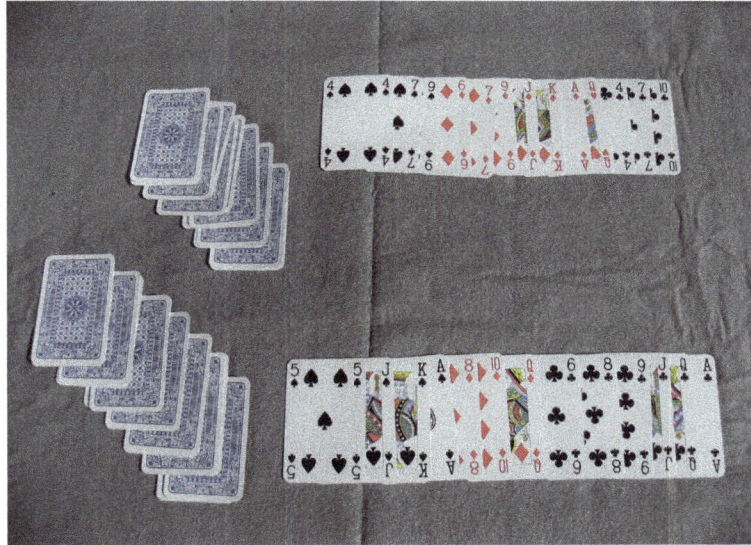

19 *German Whist* – Stage Two
On the left you can see the tricks which have been taken. The players now try to win tricks with the cards which they obtained during the first stage. Of course, they don't show each other their hands.

winner. I've always liked this game because the rules and terminology are easier to remember than those of *Cribbage* or *Piquet* – the other two popular card games for two players.

Cribbage is presumably an English game whereas *Piquet* appears to have originated in France because its terminology is in French. I learned to play both *Cribbage* and *Piquet* when I was older and at grammar school.

14 Indoor Games (4)

Another card game which I enjoyed playing when I was still quite young was a form of *Rummy*. The aim of *Rummy* is to collect groups of cards into sets or sequences. A set consists of three or more cards of the same value (e.g. three Kings or four Tens). A sequence consists of three or more cards which can be placed in consecutive order of value (e.g. Ace, Two, Three, Four; or Ace, King, Queen, Jack, Ten). Traditionally the Ace can often be played as high or low in many card games.

20 Some *Rummy* Hands
At the top there are two sets; at the bottom are two sequences.

I didn't play rummy with a pack of normal playing cards but had some very attractive cards with pictures taken from Walt Disney full-length cartoons. I believe that I had one pack of cards which featured *Jack and the Beanstalk.** A second pack may have been taken from *Snow White and the Seven Dwarves**, but I have the feeling that the cards may have featured illustrations from a film which I hadn't seen.

A similar card game was called *Happy Families*. Each family consisted of a father and mother, a son and a daughter. They had names such as *Mr. Beef, the Butcher*, and *Mr. Loaf, the Baker*. The son and daughter would be called *Master Beef, the Butcher's son*, and *Miss Loaf, the Baker's daughter*. The aim of the game was to collect the cards into family groups. I can't remember whether or not we could also collect a group of three or four fathers, wives, sons or daughters, just as in rummy.

A very different card game was entitled *Kan-U-Go*, which was suitable for two or more players. Each card was the same size as a normal playing card but displayed a letter of the English alphabet. The aim of the game was to put down several letters at a time in order to make a

21 Happy Families
(left) This was a popular children's game. The example cards shown are the Baker's Family.

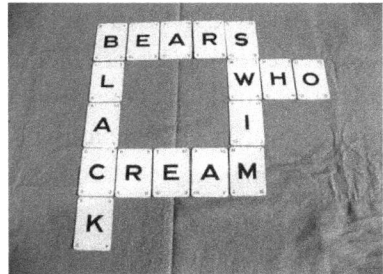

22 The Game of Kan-U-Go
This photo shows a game at the beginning.

word, but after the first word had been laid* down it was necessary to add new words in such a way as to create a pattern similar to that of a crossword puzzle (i.e. each new word had to cross another word somewhere in the pattern).*

This was a good game for people who liked reading, spelling and playing with words, but the cards took up too much space on our dining room table. I'm not surprised that *Kan-U-Go* was superseded by *Scrabble* in England during the second half of the twentieth century because the latter is played with 'tiles' which are much smaller than playing cards. The tiles used in *Scrabble* are similar to dominoes in so far that they don't become dirty and unpleasant to handle, whereas the *Kan-U-Go* cards suffered from the same defects as normal playing cards.

31

15 All Saints Church

Almost as soon as I had returned to North London, and even before I had started at St. James's School, I became involved with All Saints Church. Having been a choirboy in Somerset I must have shown interest in continuing to sing in church, because my mother's diary has an entry for Sunday 27th May 1945: *"Bernard starts in choir at All Saints."* This church was situated just over half a mile (one kilometre) up the hill from our block of flats.

It was part of the Church of England, and the Sunday morning service took place at 10.30 am. I can remember going into the vestry – a word which comes from the Latin *vestis* = which means 'clothing.' I took off my overcoat, which at that time was always a raincoat, and put on my cassock and surplice. The cassock was black and reached to my ankles; by contrast the surplice was white and reached to my knees. I had no difficulty with them because I had worn similar vestments at Dinder church.

I have only the vaguest memories of actually singing in church. I know that we would file into the choir pews and sit down. From time to time we would kneel down on our hassocks in order to pray and at other times we would stand up in order to lead the congregation in the singing of hymns.

I don't know how long I remained a choirboy, but I believe that I ceased to sing in the choir before leaving primary school. It's possible that this was an important part of my musical education, but I had no idea of that at the time.

23 All Saints Church
This is a modern photo of the church.

24 The Author as a Choirboy at All Saints
This photo was in fact taken in Wells,
Somerset, but shows me in a cassock and
surplice, the required dress for choirboys
generally in England

16 Christianity and Sunday school

A week after I had started to sing in the church choir my mother's diary has the following entry for Sunday 3rd June 1945: "Went to church 10.30am with Bernard. He went to Sunday school at 3.00 pm."

As is the case for most organised religions the Christian Church contains various schools of thought – or 'factions' as some people would say. I was brought up to think of myself as a Christian who belonged to the Church of England. This entailed my going to church on Sunday, either in the morning, or in the evening, or both. I remember very clearly that, when not singing in the choir, my church attendance was not enjoyable. The morning service lasted for about an hour, perhaps longer, and the pews were hard and uncomfortable. I enjoyed singing the hymns, but found the sermons long and rambling. The priest would stand in the pulpit and preach his sermon at great length. He had clearly spent a considerable amount of time thinking about his arguments which he put forward logically, but the premises on which he based his arguments were meaningless to me.

25 Preaching a Sermon
The priest stands in a pulpit in order to preach his sermon.

Noah's Ark

David and Goliath

26 Sunday School Stamps
These stamps (upper) are the kind
which we collected in order to stick
them into a special stamp album
(right, lower).

Every week I would breathe a sigh of relief as he reached a conclusion – only to find that he still had more to say. This would happen two or three times in one sermon and then I would have a shock when I found that he had actually finished!

It was a pleasure to come home for Sunday dinner, but after recovering from our hefty two-course meal I would have to make my way up the hill to the Sunday school which was held in a schoolroom near the church. The purpose of these lessons was to acquaint children with some of the stories in the Bible and the moral ideas which came from them. It was here that I came into close contact with various parts of the Bible.

One of the ways in which our religious teachers encouraged us to attend regularly each week, and tried to make the Bible more interesting, was to give us little stamp albums (fig. **26**). Each Sunday they would give us a stamp to stick into the album. The result was that I developed a general knowledge of the Bible when I was still quite young.

17 Scouting and the Cubs

Another activity which commenced soon after my return from Somerset was that I joined the Cubs. This organisation was an off-shoot of the Boy Scouts, which had been founded by Baden-Powell in 1908. He was an army officer who played an important part in the defence of Mafeking (1899-1900) during the Boer War in Africa. He believed that reconnaissance was important in warfare and wrote two books about the subject: "*Reconnaissance and Scouting*" (1890) and "*Aids to Scouting*" (1899). The purpose of his Scouts association was to help boys to develop good characters and a wide variety of skills such as cooking, camping, tying knots, handling small boats and so on. Eventually over sixty different badges, each one awarded if a set of skills test was passed, became available for sewing onto a scout's shirt sleeve in order to show his various skills.

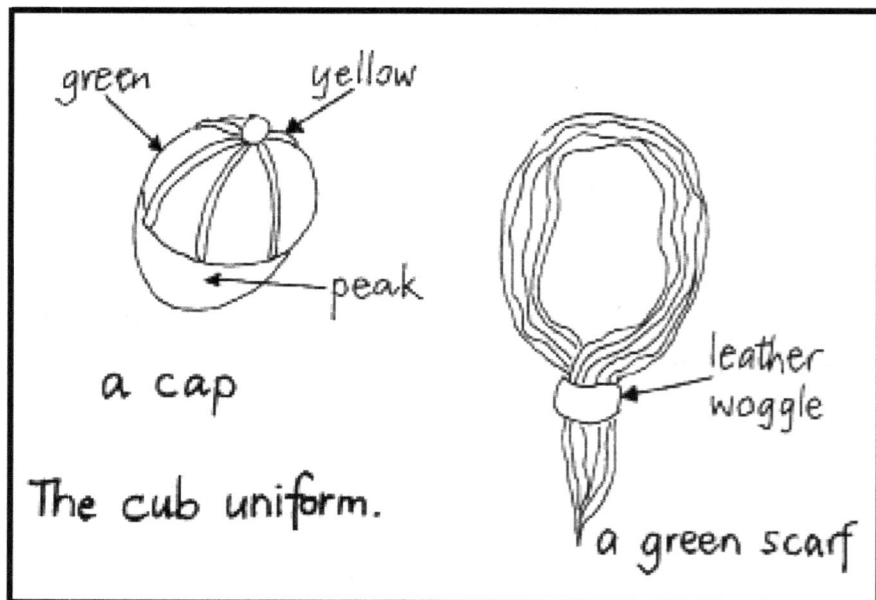

green yellow

peak

a cap

The cub uniform.

leather woggle

a green scarf

27 The Cub Uniform
We cubs wore a special cap and scarf.

A similar association, the Girl Guides, was organised by Baden-Powell and his sister a few years later, and then the Cubs (boys) and Brownies (girls) were set up in order to cater for children up to the age of eleven. These associations shared a similar Christian ethos.

28 The Scout Hut
The Scout hut was just next to Oakleigh Infants School.

My mother's diary for Saturday 2nd June 1945 has the entry: "Got Bernard Cub uniform." I may have started on the Tuesday before this, just to see what the meetings were like, but in any case I must have gone up the hill to the scout hut, just beyond All Saints Church and next to Oakleigh Infants School, on Tuesday 5th June, proudly wearing my new uniform. The basic uniform consisted of a green and yellow cap and a green scarf which was threaded through a leather ring. The latter was called a 'woggle', but who knows why? It may be that Baden-Powell made up the word by basing it on the word 'toggle.' I believe that I also tucked a small piece of green cloth (as a 'tag') into each of my garters.

18 Some Activities with the Cubs

Some of the ideas and terminology of the scouting movement came from two books by Rudyard Kipling.* He wrote a variety of books, but two of the most famous were "The Jungle Book" and "Kim."* The leaders of groups of scouts were given the names of some of the animals in the Jungle Book, and little scouts like me were called wolf-cubs.

Why did I enjoy going to the Wolf-cubs? There were several reasons. Firstly*, we often played boisterous games which enabled us to get rid of some of our youthful energy. "British Bulldog"* was one of them (**29**). It involved a few boys ('bulldogs') forming a line across the room, presumably reminiscent of the traditional British "thin red line."* The other boys had to run from one end of the scout-hut to the other, which meant forcing their way through the line. This, of course, involved a certain amount of wrestling. If a boy was prevented from breaking through the line, he joined the bulldogs. The game ended when all the boys had been captured and so had joined the line.

Secondly, we learned how to tie knots (**30**) and other practical skills.

Thirdly, we played games that encouraged us to use our brains. *Kim's Game* was just such a one (see **31** overleaf) . The idea for this game came from Kipling's book "Kim." Kim, a small boy in India, lived by his wits and on one occasion was asked to memorise a number of items on a tray. After the tray had been covered with a cloth he had to repeat back the names of the things which he had seen. We sometimes had to do the same thing in the Cubs. The idea was to make us more observant and better at recollecting things. I wonder if it had any effect on my memory!

On Sunday 24th June 1945, only a couple of weeks after I had joined the Cubs, my mother's diary has the entry: "Bernard going to

Cuffley with the cubs." This village was about six or seven miles (ten kilometres), as the crow flies, from our flat. I must have gone to a camp-site for scouts, where we would have had the chance to make fires and do some out-door cooking under the supervision of adults.

29 British Bulldog
This was a violent game but I don't remember anyone ever getting hurt.

30 A Useful Knot
The reef knot was one of several sailors' knots which we were taught. I've found it useful ever since. It has the twin advantages of not slipping and being easy to untie.

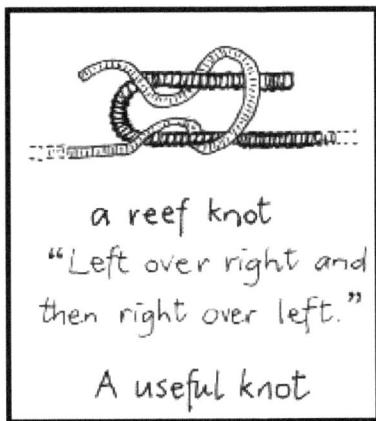

a reef knot
"Left over right and then right over left."

A useful knot

a pair of scissors

a pair of glasses

a pencil

a handkerchief

a Yale key

a magnifying glass

an old-fashioned key

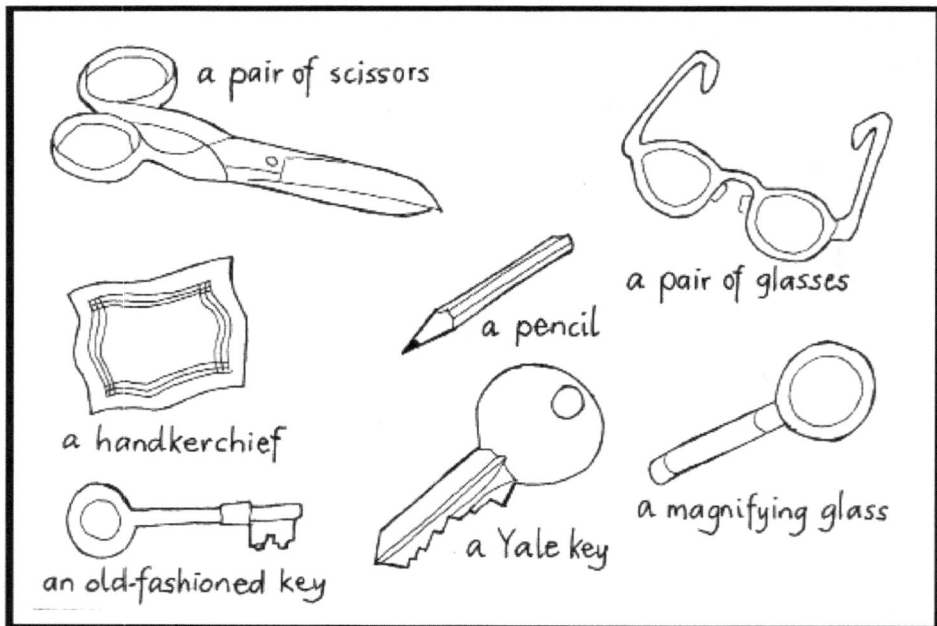

31 Kim's Game We used everyday objects for this game.

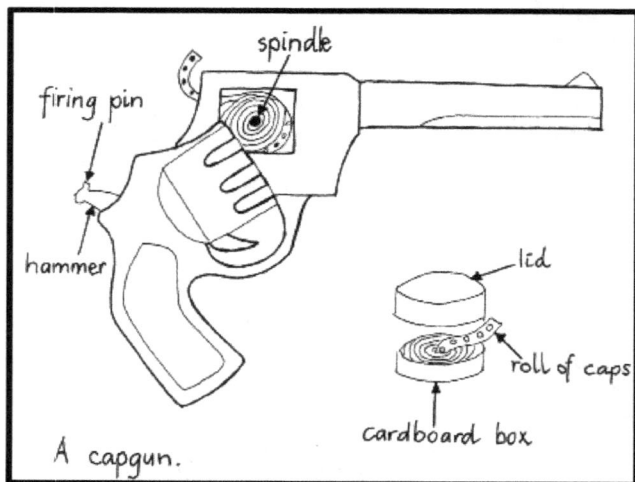

spindle

firing pin

hammer

lid

roll of caps

cardboard box

A capgun.

32 A Cap Gun
Our cap guns
looked and
sounded realistic.

19 Guns

I don't think that I'm a violent person, although I do have aggressive impulses at times, and yet toy guns were part of my childhood. This may have been the effect of American films on our culture, since the Americans still believe that their citizens have the right to carry weapons despite the huge homicide rate in the United States. A good many of the films which I saw from the age of eight until eighteen featured cowboys shooting their Colt revolvers, gunfights between cops and robbers, and detectives with their automatic pistols. After I had returned from Somerset I sometimes played such games in the street with children who lived in Marlborough Gardens.

I still have a photo which shows me at the age of about eight standing in front of the cottage porch in Dinder wearing one of Auntie Margaret's hats in imitation of a cowboy hat and holding a toy pistol. This was what we called a *cap gun* (**32**). It looked like a revolver but the cartridge cylinder was just a moulded shape and didn't revolve. You could 'open' it like a traditional revolver, but instead of six chambers into which to feed cartridges there was an empty space. This contained a spindle on which you could place a roll of 'caps' which was a thin strip of paper containing dozens of tiny explosive discs. As you pulled the trigger in order to fire the pistol, the hammer with the 'firing pin' hit a cap which exploded with a satisfying 'bang' and a mechanism moved the paper further so that you could fire the next cap.

The noise was immensely satisfying, although not in the same class as genuine Chinese fireworks, and added to the pleasure of playing Cowboys and Indians. The bad thing was that most of the boys refused to accept that they had been shot, but the good thing was that no-one ever got injured or killed!

20 ...and More Guns!

None of the guns which I handled as a child was very dangerous, although I did have a popgun (**33**) which could have caused some damage. This was a cork pistol: it used compressed air to fire corks of the kind found in wine bottles. I believe that I had to pull the handle down while holding the barrel so that a piston was pulled back inside the barrel. After pushing the handle back into position I could thrust a cork into the mouth of the barrel. When I pulled the trigger, a strong spring forced the piston to jump forward and the compressed air forced the cork out of the barrel. I enjoyed setting up some small objects, such as empty cigarette packets, and trying to hit them from a distance of two or three yards. It could have caused an injury if someone had been hit in the eye by a cork but I have never forgotten my father telling me: "Never point a gun at anyone."

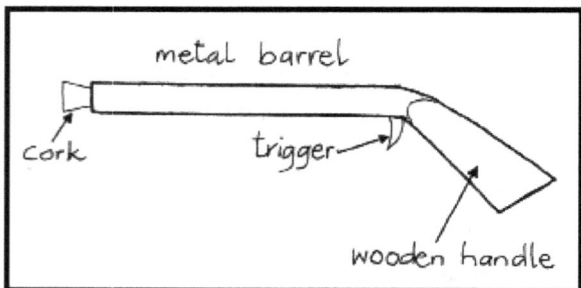

33 A Pop Gun
This had a simple mechanism which included a strong spring and it fired corks instead of bullets.

34 A Potato Gun
This was my other hand gun which fired 'bullets,' i.e. pieces of potato. These were loaded into the tip of the barrel of the gun by pressing it into a potato which thus became covered in holes.

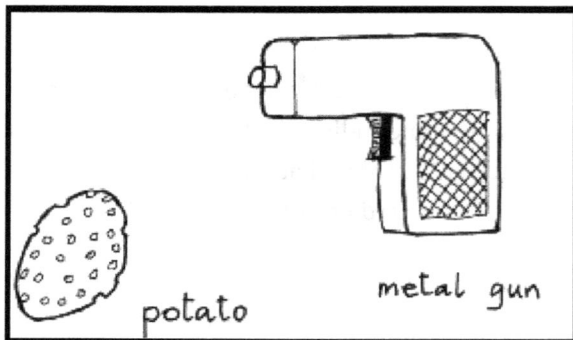

Several years later on Friday 12th March 1948 my mother's diary entry reads: "Bought potato gun for Bernard." This was a more advanced popgun which looked like an automatic and fired small pieces of potato. All that I had to do was stick the tiny tube at the end of the barrel (**34**) into a potato, to get a potato pellet in it, and then withdraw it. After I had fired a lot of potato pellets, the potato, full of surface holes, would look like a strange stone or a meteor.

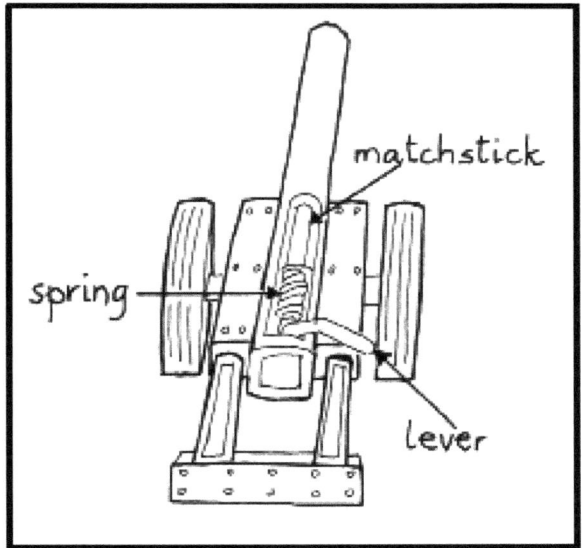

35 A Match Stick Field Gun
This fired matchsticks instead of shells.

Another gun which enabled me to shoot at targets was a toy field-gun which fired matchsticks. After the war my mother still used matches for lighting the fire in the morning and for lighting the gas-cooker. She sometimes kept the used matches for me so that I could play with them. I would put a clean matchstick into a slot in my gun and aim it towards a small object such as a matchbox. When I pressed the lever a spring forced the match along the barrel so that it flew several feet (a metre or more) through the air. Naturally I felt pleased if I managed to hit the target!

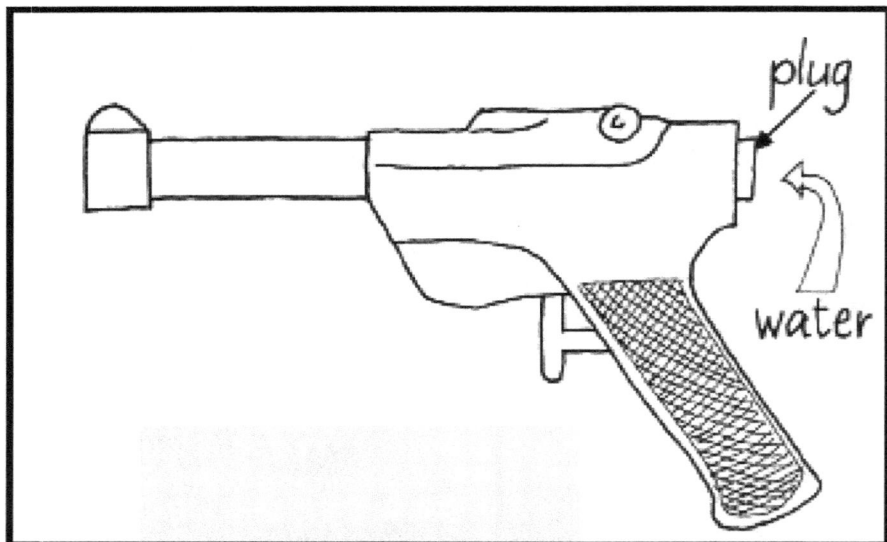

36 A Water Pistol
It was fun to squirt water and wasn't dangerous.

However, a much more exciting weapon was the water pistol! Shooting water at other boys was less dangerous and more fun than shooting other missiles - and more pleasurable in hot weather. Since those times I've never had any desire to handle guns or to shoot any living thing, but whether this is in spite of, or because of, my childhood marksmanship I really don't know.

Chapter 2

1945-1946

List of Memories

1 Friends...

Although I made a couple of close friends at primary school I have always been somewhat reserved. I enjoy being sociable, and can even become exuberant when I'm with friends, but I'm just as happy to get on with various activities by myself. Perhaps this is partly because I was an only child.

However, although I sometimes played in the street with other children who lived in Marlborough Gardens, there was a period when I felt rather lonely. I actually made the effort to look for friends at school. I seem to remember inviting Michael Lacey, and later Neil Hankin, to come for tea after school. I probably also went to have tea with them at a later date. We would have eaten bread and butter with jam, followed by cake of some kind. For a time I was friendly with another schoolmate, Brian Brooks, and on one occasion, in January 1948, he came with me to see the Bertram Mills Circus.

I seemed to get on with other people quite well for most of the time and so was invited to several parties while at primary school but my only memory of them was that my mother used to say to me, "Be a good boy, Bernard, and eat up your bread and butter before choosing cakes and jellies **(1)**. And don't forget to say, 'Thank you for having me' when you leave the party."*

I have a distinct memory that on one occasion I ate so much bread and butter that I didn't have any room left for cakes and trifle! I also remember that, at the end of my farewell speech to the staff of St. Mary's Church of England High School, Hendon, on the day of my final retirement in July 2001, I said: "Thank you for having me!"

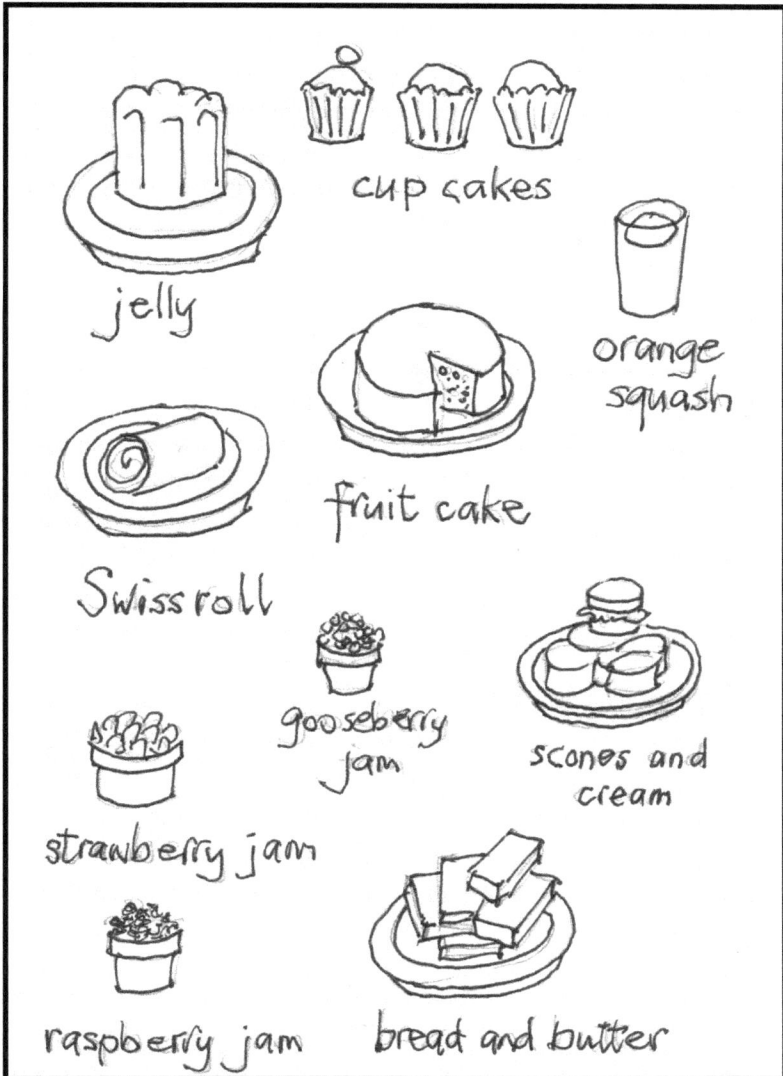

1 Party Food

2 *...and Enemies!*

I'm glad to say that I have never been bullied by a group of people. That must be very difficult to cope with. However, while I was at St. James's I was sometimes bullied by one particular boy who was bigger than me. His name was Arthur and I don't know why he chose to pick on me from time to time. Perhaps he thought that I was more fortunate than he was; or perhaps it was because I wore glasses and was fairly slim in build.

In any case he liked to come up to me and pretend to slap my face while looking smug and contemptuous at the same time. I suppose that I could just have run away but I was either too proud or too stupid to do so. In response I invariably resorted to fisticuffs and the result was often the same. He would punch me until I started to cry. However, I suppose that, rather like Oliver Twist* (**2**), I had a certain amount of pluck, and I would continue fighting until I had also made him cry. I did this by aiming to punch him in the face – being hit on the nose usually brings tears to the eyes!

Actually, we probably fought each other only half a dozen times at the most, but I also became involved in several other fights with boys both at St. James's and later once or twice at my grammar school. These were always fist-fights and were mostly lacking in expertise. As a result I learnt to stand up for myself; I never allowed someone to beat me: if I began to cry then I kept on fighting until I had made the other boy cry as well.

Indeed since that time I have never allowed anyone to bully me or treat me badly if I could help it. The only time that I remember being beaten in a fist-fight was with my cousin Ken and I got what I deserved because I had been in a bad mood!

Having said that, I should mention that Brian Smith, one of my best grammar school friends, told me many years later that he had beaten me in a fight because he 'fought dirty.' I have no memory of this. Perhaps that's because I didn't want to remember fighting a friend and then being beaten! Of course in those days we didn't kick each other because none of us had heard of Japanese Karate, French Savate, Thai Boxing or Chinese Kong Fu.*

2 Oliver Twist

3 Locomotives...

In 1945 my father owned an Ariel motorbike which he called "Freddie." On Saturday 16th June my mother wrote in her diary: "Bernard and Charles went to Malden on motorbike." I was about eight and a half years old and this was probably the first time that I went for any great distance on the pillion of my father's bike.

Our destination wasn't the Essex town of Maldon but New Malden which is situated within the Greater London area just to the south of Wandsworth and Wimbledon*, and I believe that we used the North Circular Road* as part of our route. Our purpose was to visit a model railway track.

This was not the kind of track which railway enthusiasts keep in their homes for playing with toy trains. This was far superior. It was a track running along a low concrete viaduct at a height of about one and a half feet (45 centimetres) from the ground and with a gauge of about three inches (7 centimetres). Its purpose was to provide the opportunity for a model locomotive to pull a number of passengers, seated on wheeled platforms, along the track.

Unlike the usual toy trains, which were produced by commercial firms, these locomotives were made by keen amateurs who made all their parts on a lathe. They assembled the various parts to make fully-functioning locomotives which were scale models of the real thing.

Of course, at that time all the main-line trains used coal. Electricity was used only for the London Underground. Each model locomotive was about two feet (60 centimetres) long and had its own tender in which real lumps of coal were stored. Naturally these lumps were much smaller than those which we used at home on our coal fires.

The driver used a tiny shovel to feed coal into the furnace and it was an impressive sight to see such a small train engine pulling up to twenty adults and children with their legs dangling on each side of the track.

3 The Track at New Malden

4 ...and a Lathe

I don't know whether or not my father had begun to make his own locomotive before our visit to New Malden in June 1945, but I doubt it. From several references in his 1947 diary I believe that he must have been using his own lathe in 1946.

On Sunday 2nd February 1947, after it had snowed heavily, he wrote in his diary: "Broke off using lathe to make a sledge for Bernard."

On Saturday 15th February 1947 he wrote: "Dug out loco and prepared for steam test."* This implies that he had already made the locomotive which would have been a time-consuming process over a period of several months.

On Sunday 6th April he wrote: "Last jobs on loco. pm. To track." This means that he finished work on his train-engine in the morning and took it to the track at New Malden in the afternoon.

At that time he had the lathe mounted on a bench in the little bedroom and I believe that I had my bed next to that of my parents. I do know that on Sunday 8th December 1946 my mother wrote: "Started changing Charles' room for Bernard" and my father's lathe was moved to a position next to the window in my parents' bedroom. The little room became my permanent bedroom from January 1947 until I left home in 1965.

Later, for various reasons, my father wrote on Sunday 31st January 1948: "Am going to sell lathe," and eventually, on Sunday 17th July 1949, my mother wrote in her diary: "Dick Marshall came to take lathe away."

Strangely enough, when I returned from my national service in 1957* I met and became friendly with Laurence Sparey whose father was the author of *The Amateur Lathe* - a book published in 1947 specifically to help non-professional students of mechanical engineering. I imagine that my father must have come across this publication and I know that he met Mr. Sparey several times in the late 1950s. They were creative men who had several interests in common, but they never actually became close friends.

4 A Model Locomotive at New Malden

5 My Father's Motorbikes

My father kept his motorbike in one of the garages which lay behind the flats. Two weeks after Dad and I had visited the model railway club at New Malden, my mother noted in her diary on Sunday 1st July 1945: "Charles and Bernard went to Pitsea on Freddie."

Petrol had been rationed during the war but I imagine that the restrictions had begun to be eased by the summer of 1945, although petrol rationing didn't end until Saturday 27th May 1950. Be that as it may, that Sunday in July was the first of a score of motorbike trips to my father's relatives in Essex over the next ten years, although from 1950 until 1955 we travelled by motorbike and sidecar. If she were with us my mother would sit in the sidecar and I would still need to sit on the pillion.

My final visit by motorbike was not until Sunday 26th June 1955, when I was virtually at the end of my time at grammar school.

The thirty mile trip would take us not much more than an hour, but I usually felt rather stiff at the end of it. However, it was an exhilarating experience to speed along the Southend Arterial Road* in direct contact with the air and I didn't feel any fear because my father was a careful rider.

At that time we were not required by law to wear helmets, but of course we did need to wear warm clothing. My father usually wore waders which were made of rubber and when we reached our destination I would help him to remove them. He sat down on a chair and raised his leg; I grasped the heel with both hands and wriggled it backwards and forwards until eventually his foot came loose and I could pull off the whole boot. Then I did the same to the other boot. I suppose that it was rather like a squire helping a knight to remove his armour!*

5 My Uncle Ernie and his Fiancée Doris on his Motorbike

6 Visits to Pitsea

When my father took me to see his own father and other relatives, during the period 1945-1955, we would leave the Southend Arterial Road and come the last couple of miles along country lanes in order to reach Pitsea. Proceeding along Rectory Road we turned left into the Southend Road and immediately passed a park as we travelled eastwards. Beyond this on the left side of the road was a row of houses and bungalows while on the other side there were fields stretching down to Pitsea Marsh and the River Thames.

About fifty or a hundred metres beyond the park there was a metre-wide concrete path which ran straight up the hillside between two houses. Behind the houses, and parallel to the Southend Road, was a grassy track, optimistically called Brightside Road, and then some scrubland which stretched to the crest of the hill. My father usually rode our bike up the concrete path as far as the track and then veered diagonally left across a grassy area to reach my grandfather's bungalow, Hillcrest.*

On the right-hand side of the path, and opposite Hillcrest, was Glycena,* which belonged to Uncle Dave. There were several bungalows beyond Hillcrest to the west, but there was nothing to the east of Glycena for a hundred metres or so. Then there were some more bungalows, including Kendorern,* which belonged to my Uncle Ernie. Here another grassy track led down to the main road not far from a pub, *The Bull*.

When we went to Pitsea using the bike and sidecar we had to travel up this track in order to reach *Brightside Road* and then along it to my grandfather's bungalow.

My grandfather's bungalow, and the garden which lay up-hill of it, were almost at the crest of the hill. The concrete path which ran next to Glycena made a right-angled turn to the left at the top end of Uncle Dave's garden and ran along the crest of the hill between the fences of several gardens into an avenue of trees which eventually led down to Rectory Road.

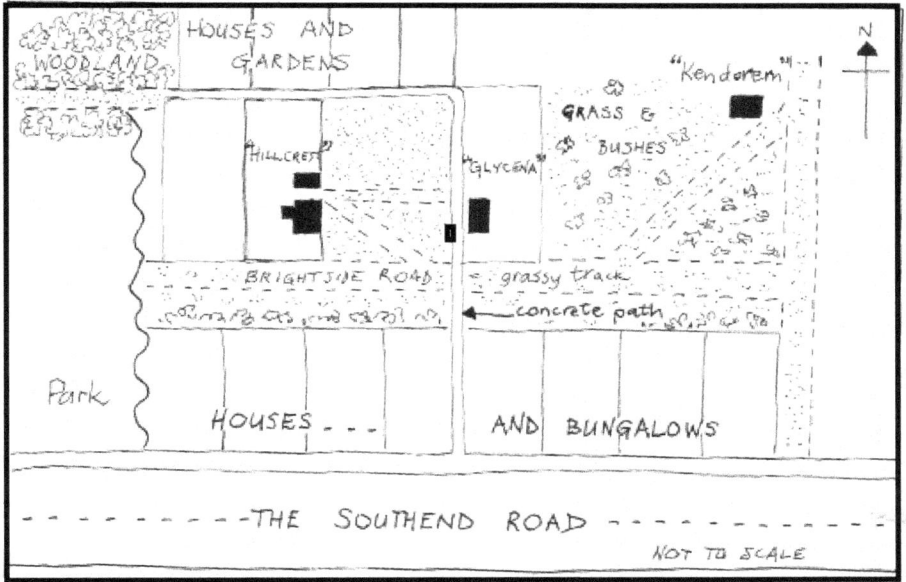

6 A Map of the Area

7 Hillcrest

Although I enjoyed our trips to Pitsea, travelling on a motorbike could be very tiring and I always felt a sense of relief when we finally arrived at my grandparents' bungalow. The front door of Hillcrest opened on to a wooden balcony, but this was always kept locked and everyone used the back door in order to enter the property. My father would steer the bike into the passage between the bungalow on the left and a row of woodsheds on the right.

After clambering down from the bike we would walk around the corner of the building, pass the window of my grandparents' bedroom and enter the tiny kitchen. The door on our left would take us into a long, narrow living room; to its left was my grandparents' bedroom and to the right, at the far end was the front door. A parallel room, the lounge, led back to a second bedroom. There was also a sofa bed in the lounge which could enable an extra couple of guests to stay overnight. We ate our meals and chatted in the living room where there were a table, some hard chairs and a couple of armchairs.

There was no bathroom or toilet. Hillcrest was similar to Church View in Dinder in so far that it had no mains sewage system, but instead of a latrine at the end of the garden there was a chemical toilet in one of the bungalow's woodsheds.

Hillcrest was also superior to Church View, not only because it had a little summerhouse at the top end of the garden instead of a privy, but because there were magnificent views over the Thames Estuary. Granddad had a very large brass and leather telescope, which I used to balance on the handle of a garden fork stuck into the lawn, so that I could gaze at the ships gliding along the river and the huge drums of the oil refinery on Canvey Island* shining in the sun.

7 *Hillcrest*

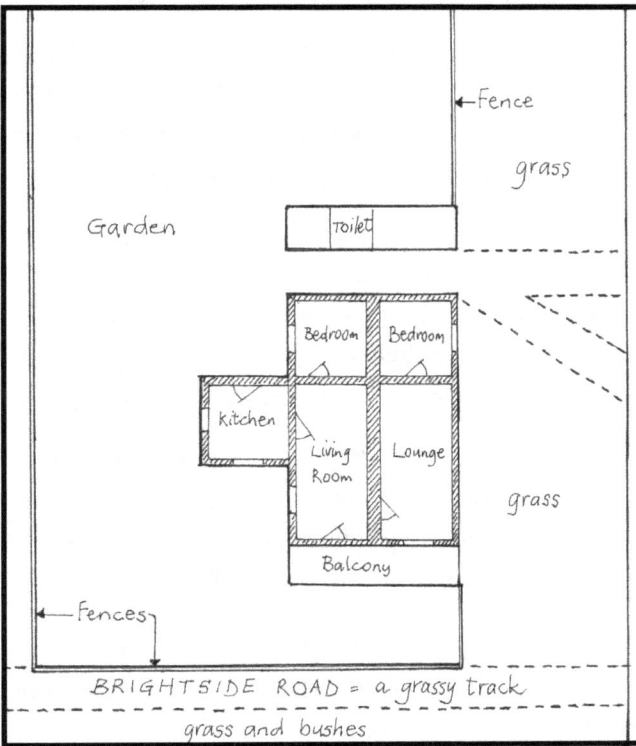

←Fence

grass

Garden

Toilet

Bedroom   Bedroom

Kitchen

Living
Room   Lounge

grass

Balcony

←Fences┐

BRIGHTSIDE ROAD = a grassy track

grass and bushes

8 A Plan of
Hillcrest

8 Entertainment at Hillcrest

As well as going to Pitsea on the occasional Sunday afternoon I also enjoyed several holidays there. I went for a week or so every Easter from 1946–1950 and also spent a week or two there in the summer holidays of 1946, 1948 and 1950. I would sleep in the bedroom at the end of the lounge, but I was able to spend the day doing more or less what I liked.

Sometimes I played with my cousin Ken over at Kendorern and sometimes with Joan and Carol who were Uncle Dave's daughters. On at least one occasion Cousin Pam, Tom's daughter, joined Joan, Carol and me. We explored the woodland at the end of the concrete path but we never reached the far end which presumably reached Rectory Road.

I was also thrilled when my Uncle Dave took me to work with him one day in April 1950 when I was thirteen years old. He allowed me to screw some socket covers into place after he had fitted the electrical wiring, and I felt that I had done something practical for a change.

What really interested me at Hillcrest was the pianola (player-piano) which stood against the exterior wall of the lounge (**11**, overleaf). A corner cupboard was filled from floor to ceiling with piano-rolls and I loved to clip a roll into the recess behind a panel above the keyboard and then start playing piano music by merely pumping two pedals.

My father liked to move a couple of small levers in order to add dynamics and some rubato to the music, but I didn't usually bother with these subtleties. The music included famous pieces of light classical music such as Overtures and Marches together with Jazz pieces from the 1920s and 1930s. Thus my musical education continued and it was probably due to the pianola that I developed an interest in playing the piano, but I didn't have the opportunity to play the piano regularly until several years later.

9 The Author (top left), Pamela (standing), Ken (sitting) with baby Colin, and Joan (sitting on a cushion) (1946?)

10 The Meadows Family and Friends Enjoying a Picnic at *Hillcrest*
The numbers in the outlines below refer to the names of each person
- or at least those I can remember!

1. Nana Meadows (née Smith)
2. Joseph Meadows
3. Unknown
4. Uncle Ernie
5. Charles Meadows
6. Uncle Dave
7. Auntie Margaret
8. Auntie Doris with Colin
9. Joan Meadows
10. Uncle Tom
11.& 12 Unknown
13 Kenneth
14 The Author

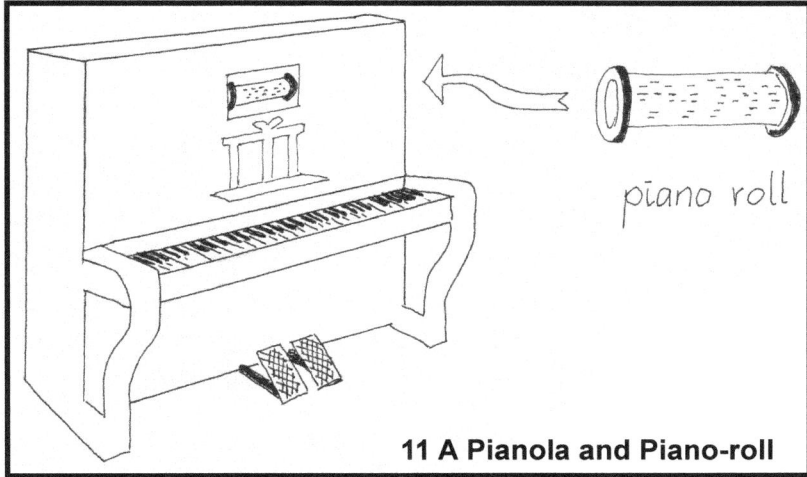

11 A Pianola and Piano-roll

The Meadows family was fortunate in so far that none of us died as a result of the Second World War (1939-1945). Joseph Meadows was a military lorry driver during the First World War (1914-1918) and was presumably not required to join the armed services in 1939. His eldest son, my father, Charles, was also not required to join up because he was involved in the important task of developing Radar.

I have the impression that my father's brother, my uncle Ernie, spent some time in India during the war. He may have been in the Royal Electrical and Mechanical Engineers. Uncle Tom was a member of the Artillery but I know nothing about his wartime experiences. Nana was Joseph's second wife and my uncle Dave was her only son and the youngest of the brothers. He was a member of the Royal Air Force and became Flight Engineer on Sunderland Flying Boats which operated across the Atlantic. He visited both Iceland and Ireland, and he met Margaret in the latter country. She became his wife and their baby daughter, Joan, is sitting next to them in the photo. Uncle Dave, and later Uncle Tom, took their families to New Zealand in the early 1960s.

9 *Southend*

Southend lies on the left bank of the River Thames about thirty-five or forty miles to the east of London. It's a popular seaside resort for Londoners, especially those in the East End of London,* and is famous for its pier which is over a mile long. When I first visited it there was a small train with open-air carriages which ran from the shore out to the end of the pier. Some people liked to walk to the end of the pier and take the train back. There were four possible permutations of getting to the end of the pier and returning, but all of them involved coming into contact with the sea breezes - the allegedly healthy ozone.

I don't know for sure when I first went to Southend. It may well have been when I spent a week with Nana and Granddad in April 1946, or it may have been when I stayed with them in August of the same year, but I certainly went to Southend for the first time on a Sunday school outing on Friday 19th July 1946.

The promenade stretched for several hundred yards and provided a wide variety of 'attractions.' There were amusement-arcades which offered a multitude of opportunities to use and lose one penny at a time. There were sea-food kiosks selling winkles, whelks and jellied eels (popular with the East Enders), cafés and restaurants. There was even the *Kursaal* (pronounced 'kerzl' in English), coming from the German for 'spa hall,' which was like a shopping arcade for entertainment.

I enjoyed climbing up the stairs of the *helter-skelter* tower (**12**) with my mat, on which I sat in order to slide round and round to the bottom; sometimes I was able to stop a little way before the bottom and climb back up the slide so that I could have another go.

Most enjoyable of all, however, were the *dodgems* (**13**), which were electric cars with bumpers so that people could enjoy bumping into each other. They were also called *bumper cars*. I liked to avoid colliding with the other cars and it was on the dodgems that I first learned to drive!

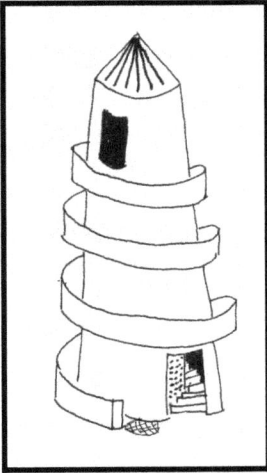

12 A Helter-Skelter

13 *Bumper cars*
Also called *dodgems.*

10 My Bicycle

I mentioned in my previous memory that I loved driving the dodgems at Southend. Such a car could turn on the spot and I took a pride in looking ahead and seeing the potential hazards. Whereas most people liked crashing into each other I would see how long I could avoid colliding with someone else. As a result my road sense developed at an early age although I didn't begin to drive a car until I was about twenty-five.

I rode a tricycle for a time while still quite young and this must have given me a good grounding in the basic movements of steering and pedalling.

14 The Author on His Tricycle

My parents must have given me a bicycle for my ninth birthday in November, or for Christmas, 1945, because on Sunday 17th February 1946 my mother wrote: "Bernard rode his bike in afternoon after Sunday school."

Later in the year, on Saturday 12th October, I went to the Barnet Odeon for a Police Quiz about cycling and road safety; I did well enough to be given a free pass to visit the cinema and so went there the following Saturday afternoon.

I remember that my father helped me to get started in the courtyard behind our flats, then down the slope to Marlborough Gardens and around the corner into the service road. He held on to the back of the saddle and this gave me the confidence to pedal and remain upright.

After a short while he told me that he had ceased to hold the saddle and therefore I had been cycling by myself! After that I had no difficulty without his help - except that I fell off a few times trying to get the hang of making a tight turn to one side or the other at the end of the service road.

I sometimes went to school by bike and only ceased to use it after I had left home to do my National Service.*

11 A Cold Winter

Although I went cycling in February 1946, my mother's diary for Sunday 3rd March contained two words: "Deep snow." It was probably at this time that I made an attempt to build an igloo in the courtyard behind the flats.

I'm not sure how I constructed it, though I believe that it was possible for me to crawl into it. I do know that I tried to imitate the snow house of the Eskimos, or *Inuit* as they are now known. I doubt whether I was in any great danger if it had collapsed on me, as it was very small and didn't have the traditional tunnel entrance of the igloos which we see in pictures.

I enjoyed going out into the cold and the snow because it seemed adventurous, but of course I was always glad to get back into the warm. We boys liked to play with snowballs and they weren't really dangerous when we made them with soft, freshly-fallen snow, but they were potentially dangerous when the old snow became icy.

Fortunately I don't remember ever suffering from being hit by a snowball.

What is remarkable is that I must have been wearing short trousers! It was the custom for small boys and young teenaged boys to wear short trousers and I didn't graduate to long trousers until Sunday 11th December 1949, when I was in my second year at grammar school. I don't know why we wore short trousers when we were young; it wasn't the custom in the nineteenth century. It might have been because of the Boy Scout movement and the idea that it was good to get fresh air on your legs. Also, I suppose that short trousers cost less than long ones.

15 Igloos

12 Rationing

In the winter after the war had ended we didn't just suffer from some very cold weather. We also continued to endure the rationing of sweets, clothing and essential foodstuffs. Rationing had been introduced as a response to the problems of obtaining food and raw materials. We depended on our merchant navy to bring us many things which we couldn't produce ourselves and our shipping had suffered badly from attacks by German submarines.

I still have our last set of *ration books*, one each for my father, mother and me. They covered the period from 17th May 1953 until the week ending 15th May 1954.

The first pages contained coupons for Meat, Eggs, Fats (e.g. butter and margarine), Cheese, Bacon and Sugar. The grocer would scribble with a pencil over the coupons which had been used. Then came a page for Tea. After this there are several pages with symbols for which I don't know the purpose. I do know that we had coupons which we needed if we wanted to buy clothes, but the clothing coupons are not listed as such. I think that they were in a separate booklet. Then there are two pages of sweet coupons, which needed to be cut out. A note at the top of the page states: "Do not cut out coupons. The shopkeeper will do this for you." I believe that we also had bread coupons during the war, but these were no longer needed in 1953.

Several times my mother comments in her diaries: "Filled in new ration books." This refers to the fact that it was necessary to write your name and address on a form at the front of the book. A note also stated: "ENTER names and addresses of Retailers." Our butcher's name was Atkinson, who was located underneath our flats next to our baker, and our grocer was situated on the opposite side of Oakleigh Road. We didn't need to go far for our basic supplies.

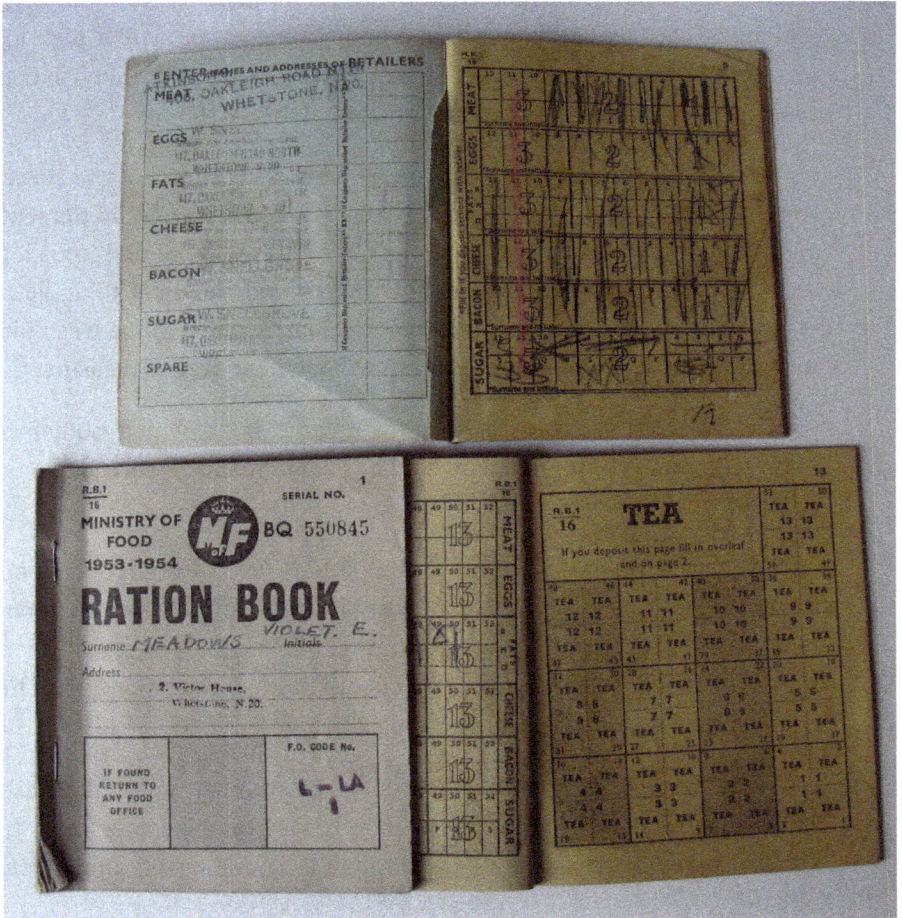

16 Our Ration Books

13 Fun with Cardboard

Despite the problems which came with the war, such as rationing, my childhood was generally speaking a happy time. I remember learning to use scissors in order to cut pieces out of cardboard which I then assembled into three-dimensional objects.

At one time I was able to create a castle by cutting out the pieces from several sheets of card on which were printed the walls, battlements and turrets. Each piece of card had a tab or tabs which fitted into slots on another piece. There were also letters and numbers to indicate where each piece fitted into the structure. The whole edifice was quite imposing and this kind of activity gave me a great deal of pleasure.

The castle may have come from a large book which contained numerous sheets of printed card so that I could make all sorts of things with very little effort.

I remember in particular a flat crocodile. After cutting it out, I bent down the two flaps at its sides, placed a cotton reel between them and pushed a knitting needle, or something like that, through one flap, through the hole in the cotton reel, and out through the other flap. This enabled me to roll the crocodile along a flat surface.

There were other things which could be made using matchsticks, rubber bands, acorns and conkers. It was easy to make a teetotum by sticking a match or similar object through the middle of a round piece of card.

This kind of activity encouraged me to use my hands without the need for higher level carpentry skills. Of course, in my younger days, I had a lot of help from my mother.

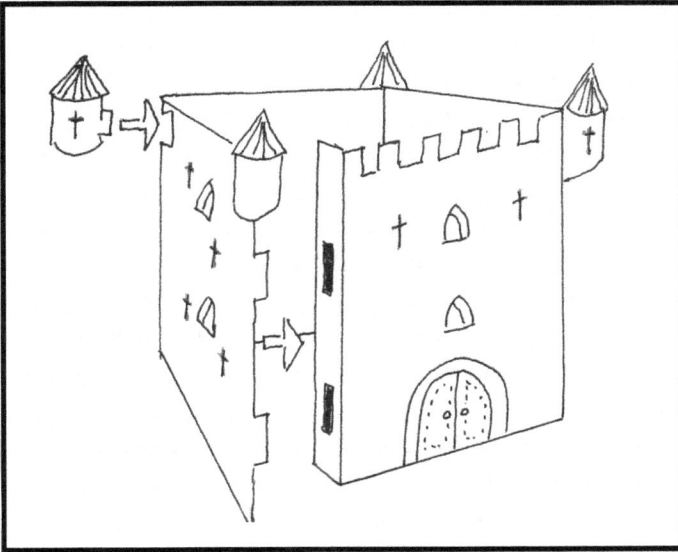

17 A Cardboard Castle

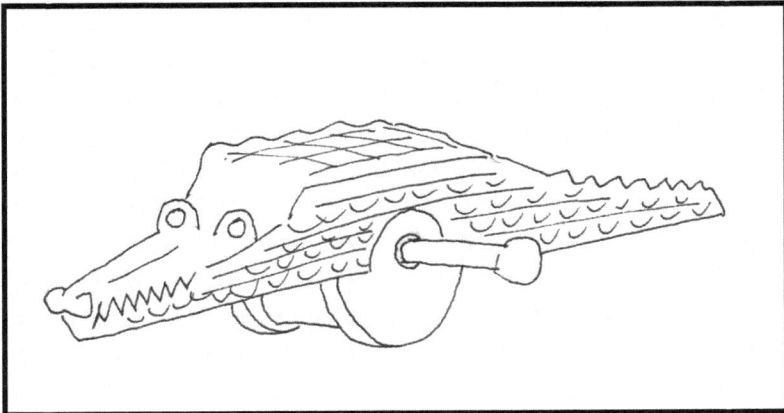

18 A Toy Crocodile

14 Cigarette Cards

For a short time I enjoyed playing a game at my primary school which involved cards which were different from normal playing cards. This game was called *Flickers* and it was played with cigarette cards.

Before the Second World War various cigarette companies were highly successful at advertising their products and one way that they did this was to include an attractive little card in each packet of cigarettes. Each card was part of a series, and the smoker was encouraged to buy more packets of cigarettes in order to stand a chance of acquiring more cards from the series. There must have been dozens of series and hundreds of different illustrations on the cards. They featured such subjects as Cars, Soldiers, Flags and Animals. It was also possible to obtain albums in which to stick the cards.

I was given a shoe box* full of cigarette cards by Mr. Miles who lived at the end of our balcony – perhaps because at that time he didn't have any children.

I began to take some of them to St. James's so that I could play *Flickers* with some other boys. We would squat down two or three yards (metres) from a wall and one boy would flick a card so that it fell at, or near, the base of the wall. This involved holding the card between the index and middle fingers and then throwing it horizontally. The next boy would then flick a card in the hope that it would touch, or partly cover, the first card. So it went on until a boy was able to make his card cover part of one or more of the other cards; he then won all the cards which were lying on the ground. After picking up the cards which he had won he would then start the next game by flicking another card towards the wall.

I lost a lot of cards that way, but as my mother used to say, "Easy come, easy go!"

19 *Flickers*

15 Conkers

I mentioned conkers in a previous memory. They are the inedible nuts of the horse chestnut tree which are enclosed in a spiky green covering. When I was young, many boys played the game of *Conkers* which involved striking one conker with another.

First of all we had to collect some conkers to play with. We would make our way to where there were some *conker trees* and look for windfalls, i.e. conkers which had been blown down by the wind.

We broke open the tough, green covering in order to get at the conker inside, but very often the coverings had already split and there were lots of conkers lying around. If we were impatient because there were no conkers to be seen on the ground, we would throw sticks at the branches in the hope of knocking some conkers down. We usually met with limited success!

We then went home and drilled a hole through each conker, through which we threaded a piece of string. We tied a big knot at one end so that the conker wouldn't fall off the string.

The game was played like this. Boy A let his conker dangle like a spider at the end of his string. Boy B held his own string firmly and hit his conker as hard as he could against the other one. He was allowed one strike. Then Boy A took his turn to hit his opponent's conker. So it went on until one or other of the conkers broke into pieces.

A keen player would remember how many conkers he had broken. If he broke his first conker he would say, "My conker's a one-er." If Boy A had a fiver and Boy B had a three-er, whoever won would be able to say, "My conker's an eight-er." It was a time-consuming game and I only played it a few times.*

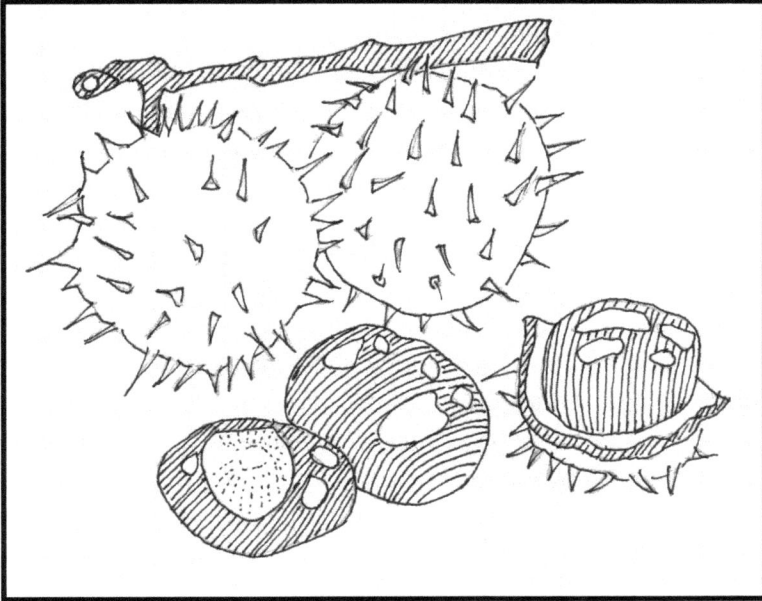

20 Conkers

21 Playing Conkers

16 Transfers and Funny Faces

At some time while I was at St. James's I was introduced to the idea of sticking pictures on to my arm or wrist in order to pretend that I was wearing a tattoo. This was another popular pastime among some of the boys at the school.

We bought *transfers* at the local newsagent. Each one consisted of a brightly coloured picture on a thin film. I put the transfer face down on my arm, wrist or the back of my hand and then made it wet – usually by licking it! After waiting for a little while I could gently peel away the backing film and there was a splendid tattoo. The good thing was that I didn't have to wear it for the rest of my life. Indeed, this was a craze which lasted for only a few weeks.

At that time very few people wore tattoos. This was mainly the custom of sailors who had been in the Merchant Navy.* However, by the beginning of the 21st century tattooing had become widespread in the London area, and there were several tattoo parlours in the Barnet area.

In the Spring of 2013 I bought a booklet of transfers (© 1995) which was entitled *Celtic Tattoos* and inside the cover it called them "temporary tattoos based on ancient Celtic designs." It seems that in the space of half a century transfers had become known as t*emporary tattoos*.

Our artistic activities at Primary school weren't restricted to sticking transfers onto our wrists. Fred Murphy, John Browne and I developed a game which involved one of us drawing a rough shape on paper. John, in particular, enjoyed producing the shape by making a kind of scribble. One of the others would change it into the picture of a face. Between us we would then give it a silly name, which was meant to reflect the person's character.

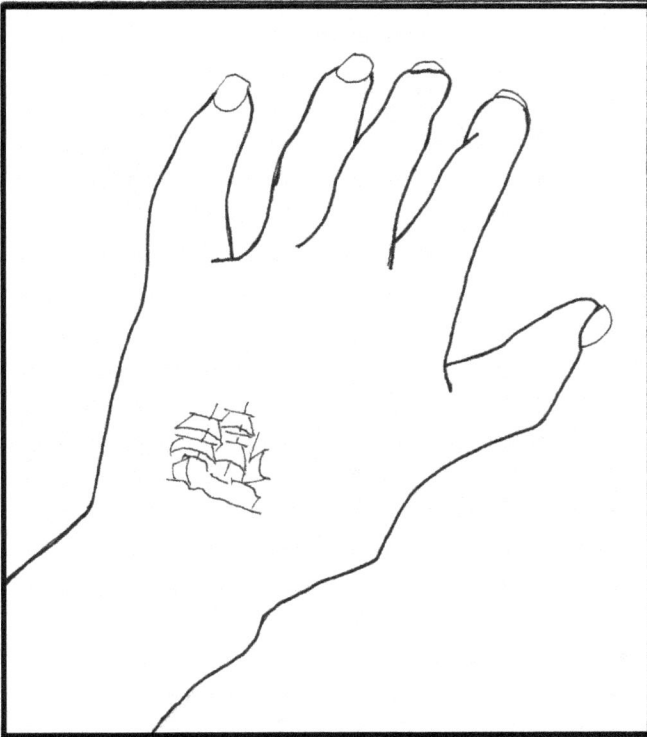

22 A Transfer on My Hand

17 Swings & Roundabouts

I began to go to the *swings* when I was quite young. This was a general term for various pieces of apparatus found in some public parks, which were also known as *recreation grounds*.

There were swings at a recreation ground in Oakleigh Road only a few hundred yards east of our flats and some more swings at Friary Park, which was situated in Friern Barnet Lane, just south-east of the North Middlesex Golf Course. At each site there were swings, a roundabout, a slide, a rocking horse, a seesaw and a climbing frame.

The individual swings consisted of four or five wooden seats in a row, each suspended by two chains from a common metal frame. Some of the seats had wooden slats around them so that smaller children could be seated more safely (see the seat on the right in **23**). A parent or other child would push the person on the swing although it was possible for you to make the seat swing backwards and forwards by yourself. It often involved a great deal of screaming!

There was also a communal swing which could seat about four children with one child standing at each end. They sat on a thick wooden plank with a ring set in the wood for each child to hold on to. Those standing at each end would pull on the supports in order to set the swing in motion.

The *roundabout* was a round platform which could spin on its axis. One roundabout's platform was only about four inches (ten centimetres) off the ground and we could only stand on it; the other one had a running board on which we could stand, and it also provided a raised platform on which we could sit. This was about two feet (sixty centimetres) higher than the running board. No matter what kind of roundabout it was, we liked to set it in motion and then jump on and off. It was dangerous but we didn't worry unduly!

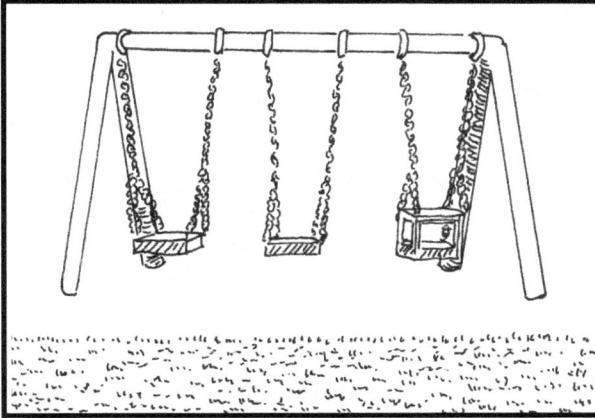

23 Single *Swings*

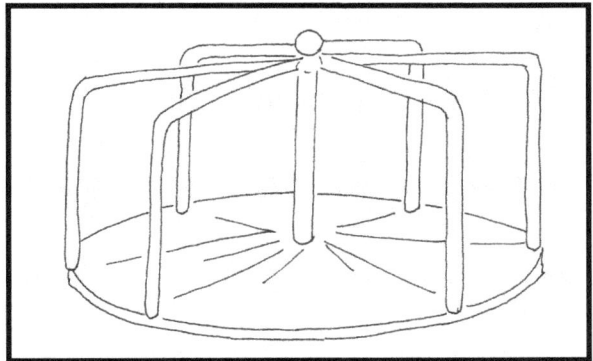

24 A Platform *Roundabout*

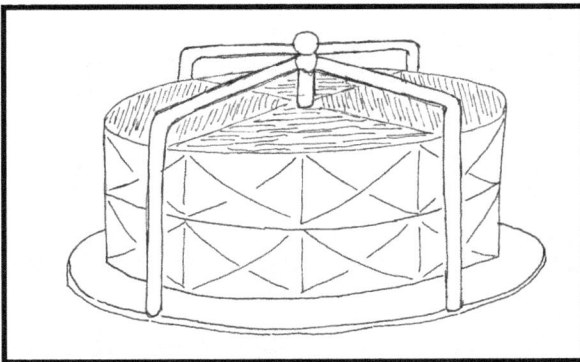

25 A *Roundabout* **with Seats**

18 More Play Apparatus

The *slide* was another piece of apparatus at the playground and one which could be dangerous. It consisted of a set of steps or a ladder leading up to a small platform on which you could sit. In front of you was the smooth slope of a metal slide which extended for three or four yards and ended horizontally for a yard or so. It had a slight wall on each side in order to keep you from falling sideways off the slide.

Unlike the helter-skelter at Southend there wasn't a mat to sit on, nor to land on at the end of the slide. The one at Friary Park wasn't very smooth at the end and so children stopped automatically, but the one at the Oakleigh Road recreation ground consisted of highly polished brass and we went shooting off the end. We had to be able to stand up and run a few paces as we left the slide!

Sometimes a group of us played a game called *Keep the Kettle Boiling*. Once we had slid down the slide we had to run back to the steps and mount them as quickly as possible so that there was no gap between one child and the next. This was quite good for making us breathless!

Each playground also contained a *rocking horse*. This was different from the rocking horses which wealthy people could buy for their children. A family rocking horse was made of wood and the best ones looked like a real horse; their four legs stood on two curved runners, known as 'rockers,' and a boy or girl could sit on such a horse and pretend to be riding it.

The ones in the playground consisted of a long wooden platform which could hold about four children. The front part looked like the head of a horse, but each child sat holding on to a ring on the back of the 'saddle' of the one in front of him or her.

The horse moved backwards and forwards more or less in a straight line with a slight rocking movement, and it helped if an adult pushed it, although it was possible for us to get it moving by ourselves by using our arms and legs.

26 The Author on a Slide

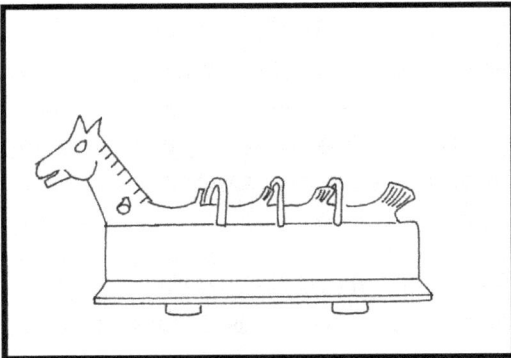

27 A Playground Rocking Horse

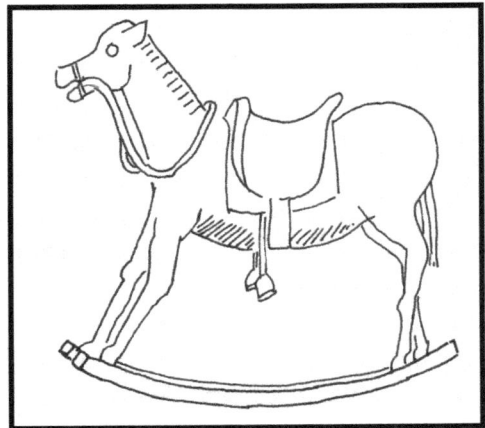

28 A Family Rocking Horse

85

19 Some More Play Apparatus

There was something at most recreation grounds which was not very dangerous – the *seesaw*. This was a thick and heavy plank of wood with two large metal rings, each one set into the wood a foot or so from each end, so that a child could sit astride the plank and grasp the ring.

The plank was pivoted on a support in the middle which acted as a fulcrum: when one end of the plank was on the ground, the other end was raised about four feet (120 centimetres) from the ground. This could only function when there were two children, but sometimes a brave or foolhardy boy would walk up the seesaw to the middle and then move the plank up and down by shifting his weight!

Usually however there were two participants who faced each other. The child at the bottom would push downwards with his or her legs so that the end rose into the air and, when the other end was low enough, the other child did likewise. This resulted in a 'seesaw motion' by the plank. It seems to have been quite an ancient device which wasn't very dangerous, but it could be uncomfortable if the plank hit the ground too hard!

The most dangerous item at any playground, however, was probably the climbing frame. This consisted of a large number of iron or steel bars, each about two feet (sixty centimetres) long, which fitted together: four bars made a square shape, twelve bars made the outline of a cube, and the whole structure might consist of fifty or sixty such cubes which were joined together into a massive cube which was set into the ground.

It was great fun to climb in and out, and up and down this structure, but there was no special elastic surface underneath to soften the fall if someone slipped.

At some time after the Second World War the authorities began to consider the importance of 'Health and Safety'* in relation to children's playgrounds. I expect that this lessened the number of bruises and broken bones. I was fortunate in that I never injured myself while playing on the swings and in the park, but I always enjoyed myself and I certainly got plenty of exercise.

29 The Author on a Climbing Frame

20 Swimming

Another activity which was very beneficial to me was that I learned to swim while at Junior School. On Thursday 30th October 1946 my mother's diary records: "Bernard swimming and cubs as usual."

School swimming lessons probably commenced for me in the previous September when I was just under ten years old. We used to be taken by coach to Bowes Road Swimming Pool, which is now called Arnos Swimming Pool and lies only a couple of hundred yards east of Arnos Grove Underground Station. We went into a changing room through a door on the right of the entrance, changed into our swimming trunks and then went through a door at the far end of the room. Here we gathered at the pool side to be told what to do.

These lessons were always enjoyable. I can't remember all the details, but non-swimmers practised at the shallow end and started by holding onto a bar at the edge of the pool with our arms stretched out. We then kicked our legs up and down as vigorously as possible. The next stage was for us to hold onto a large piece of cork while kicking our legs as before. This seemed to go on for some weeks or months. Eventually we were allowed to swim without a cork while doing dog-paddle with our hands and forearms, but I always kept the big toe of one foot safely on the bottom.

One day I suddenly noticed that I didn't have a foot on the bottom and I realised that I was actually swimming. After that I was able to make moderate progress without ever becoming a really good or keen swimmer.

After changing back into our clothes it made us feel more cheerful when we were able to buy a mug of hot Bovril. The makers claimed that it was made from beef-extract and it was meant to restore our energy for the trip back to school. My mug of Bovril always seemed to take a long time before it was cool enough to drink, and so I usually burnt my mouth in my hurry to get ready for the climb back on to the coach!

30 Bowes Road Swimming Pool

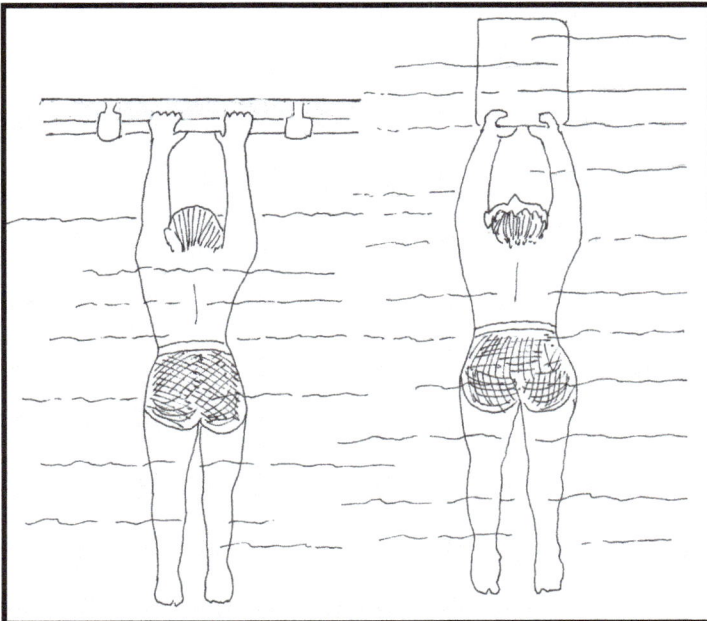

31 *Left* Holding on to the Side of the Pool. *Right* Holding on to a Cork Float

Chapter 3

1947

List of Memories

1. Football

2. Libraries and a Book Club

3. Encyclopaedias

4. My Father's Curriculum Vitae (1)

5. My Father's Curriculum Vitae (2)

6. Talking Books

7. Leicester

8. Dad's Practical Skills

9. My Parents' Health

10. Cigarettes

11. ..and Smoking

12. Chain Smoking

13. My Health

14. My Mother at Standards

15. Mother's Friends at Standards

16. A Silly Mistake

17. My Chores

18. London Zoo

19. The Circus

20. Christmas 1947

1 *Football*

I began to play football at St. James's as part of the school curriculum and this continued until I left grammar school at the age of eighteen. Once a week we used to change into our football kit in our classroom and then walk around to the playing field behind the school. Our kit included proper football boots, and I believe that we played football in this way only during my two years with Miss Leroy.

On Wednesday 22nd October 1947 my mother's diary has the entry: "Bought football boots for Bernard. 24/1d" This meant twenty-four shillings and a penny, in other words £1-4-1d. (In words, one pound, four shillings, and one penny.) Today this would be £1-20, but of course money was worth more then. In October 1947 my father's monthly salary was £39-17-8d, which would be almost £39-90 in decimal currency*, and so the purchase of these boots was an expensive item.

I enjoyed playing football and sometimes took my boots with me to play with a few other boys in Bethune Park, which lay only a few hundred yards down the hill from our flat. I sometimes played with two of my classmates: Arthur Jewell who lived in Russell Road (not very far from John Browne, see *Postscript*, who never showed any interest in football) and Richard (Dickie) Messer who lived in one of the prefabs* next to Bethune Park.

It was our custom to use a couple of jackets as 'goal posts' and on one occasion I forgot to take my jacket home with me. I strolled wearily home but when my mother said, "Where's your jacket?" I panicked and ran straight back to look for it. Fortunately it was still lying where I had left it, but I'm sorry to say that I've always been somewhat absent-minded. There have been many times when I've left something behind me!

"The beautiful game", as football is sometimes called, was also a popular pastime in the school playground, but we used a tennis ball which was easier to control than a full-sized football, and our teams were larger than just eleven.

As I grew older, however, my enthusiasm declined, partly because I was interested in so many other things. Eventually I reached the stage where I had very little interest in either playing or watching the game. I suppose that I could now say, "Football leaves me cold."

1 The Author with a Football

2 Libraries and a Book Club

Although I enjoyed physical activities, reading was important to me from an early age. I remember how Miss Leroy allowed her pupils to stop work one by one so that we could go to choose a book from her class library at the side of the class. Even before I began to attend grammar school I was learning a lot about history and geography just by reading adventure stories, but strangely enough, it wasn't until I was just over ten years old that I first joined a public library.

On Saturday 18th January 1947 I went to join Friern Barnet Library, which was about three-quarters of a mile away (one and a half kilometres) from our flat. I had to bring a form home for my parents to sign, after which I received two cardboard tickets with my name and address on them.

It became my custom to walk down Oakleigh Road past the Allotment Gardens and then along a road which led down to Bethune Park through the prefabs. I walked along a path through Bethune Park, along Bethune Avenue and Crescent Road, up Glenthorne Road and then along Friern Barnet Road to the library. Sometimes I would ride my bike along the same route, and occasionally I would borrow a book for my mother or father, as well as for myself.

A year later, on 24th January 1948, my mother joined Foyle's Book Club which was based in the Charing Cross Road. This thoroughfare was famous in the 20th century for its bookshops selling new and second-hand books. She paid a modest subscription each year and every month was sent a list of novels from which she could choose one.

Over the years she filled a bookcase with these volumes which were by modern authors such as Nevil Shute, Doris Lessing, Georgette Heyer and Peter Cheyney. I also read some of them for myself and can still remember reading *Randall and the River of Time* by C.S. Forester and *Berlin Hotel* by Vicki Baum. Even before I was a teenager I was reading a combination of children's stories and adult novels.

2 Friern Barnet Library

1 Victor House

2 Allotments

3 Prefabs

4 Pig Farm (smelly!)

5 Bethune Park

6 Holly Park School

7 Friern Barnet Library

8 Friern Barnet Town Hall

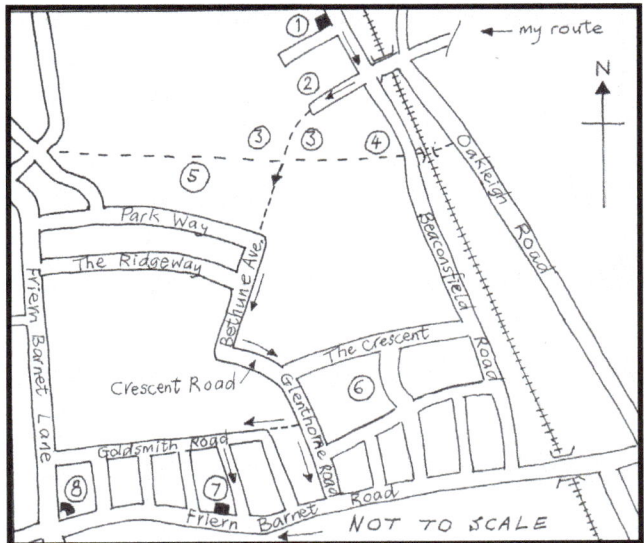

3 Map of the Library Area

3 Encyclopaedias

As an avid reader I was extremely fortunate, not only because our area was well provided with libraries, but also because my father purchased a set of encyclopaedias when I was only nine years old.

A salesman called on my parents in May 1946 with information about the *Waverley New Book of Knowledge*. There were eleven volumes in all: nine volumes of general information from A-Z, a Fact Index, and a War Supplement which was about the Second World War. My father paid £12-12-0 for them (£12.60) by hire purchase. They were usually delivered in batches of three and we received four deliveries in the space of sixteen months, from 7th October 1946 until February 1948. I suppose that each set of three books must have cost about twice as much as my football boots had done!

I can still remember my delight when each package arrived and the thrill of opening up each volume. I would sit and browse my way through each one, reading many of the texts under the pictures, maps and photographs, and occasionally reading about a topic more deeply.

I didn't look at them and then discard them; on the contrary I referred to them again and again, and their factual content made a welcome contrast to the adventure stories which I enjoyed reading. I'm sure that my easy access to these volumes of information was very beneficial during my last two years at junior school and the whole of my time at grammar school.

In the 21st century I still have them and they are lined up on the top shelf of the bookcase on the right-hand side of the window in our front room. Although much of the information is out of date, I still enjoy looking at some of their articles from time to time.

4 My Encyclopaedias
They are on the top shelf on the left.

4 My Father's Curriculum Vitae (1)

As I mentioned before, my father told me very little about his work, but in 2010 I discovered his typewritten CV* for the period 1921 until July 1949. In the latter year he was forty-three years old. Under the heading of *Education* he had listed:

> Elementary School, plus Evening Classes at
>> Ilford County High School,
>
> Southend Technical Institute,
>> and Leicester College of Technology;
>
> Also a Course on Radar at the Telecommunications Research
>> Establishment.

He went on to state: "During the 32 years covered by the statement, consistent home study has been maintained."

It appears that in 1921, at the age of fifteen, he started work as a Trainee at the *Sterling Telephone & Electric Company Limited*, Dagenham. He was involved with the assembly, inspection and testing of original Marconiphone Broadcast Receivers being made by the Sterling Company under contract.

Then from 1925 – 1927 he worked at the Amalgamated Press Ltd. in Farringdon Street, London, E.C.4. He was a technical journalist who constructed and tested equipment to be described in such journals as 'Popular Wireless' and 'Modern Wireless', as well as writing articles about such equipment.

He went on to work at *E.K. Cole Ltd.* at Southend-on-Sea from 1928 -1931. Here he was Foreman of Test and was still concerned with radio apparatus.

From 1931 – 1934 he was a Test Engineer at *Electric & Musical Industries Ltd.* at Dagenham.

He went to work for *British Acoustic Films Ltd.* from 1934 – 1936, where he was a Test Engineer (Recording), and then he was Chief Recording Engineer at British Ozaphone from 1936 – 1938. It was after he lost this job that his career changed direction.

5 A Hurricane Taking Off During the Battle of Britain

My father's work with radar was part of the defence system which helped to save Britain in 1940. See Memory 5. Notice the green and brown camouflage markings on the fuselage.

5 My Father's Curriculum Vitae (2)

My mother once told me that my father had been out of work for several months and that they had lived on her savings while he attended a course on radar. This must have been in 1938 when *British Ozaphone* closed down their Recording Department.

After my parents married in December 1935 they moved into a modern block of flats in the spring of 1936. This was Hastings House in West Ealing.

At some time after I was born we moved to Greenford, probably because this residence was only a mile or two from the Ozaphone factory in Perivale – presumably situated on Western Way. According to my father's CV he went to work in the AID (Aeronautical Inspection Directorate)* as an Examiner from 1938 – 1941 and then as a Senior Examiner from 1941 – 1943.

He had to commute several miles in order to work at *Standard Telephone and Cables* in New Southgate, and I believe that this must have continued for well over a year before we made the move to Whetstone in March 1940.

Although our flat was in Whetstone, and Standard's was in New Southgate, the factory was situated opposite our flat. It lay just beyond the main railway line from King's Cross to Peterborough and was only two or three hundred metres from our flat as the crow flies. My father could walk to work down Oakleigh Road, over the road bridge, and then left and through the extensive grounds of the factory to his office. Even though he walked slowly it probably took him only a quarter of an hour or twenty minutes to reach his office.

In 1943 he became an Assistant Inspector at *AID Central Headquarters* and had to travel up to town on the underground. From

1945 until 1949 he was Chief Examiner and I believe that he continued in this post until he retired in 1970. On at least one occasion he visited Paris for a week or so in connection with his work, and in 1962 he spent about ten weeks in Iran at the time when it was still ruled by the Shah.

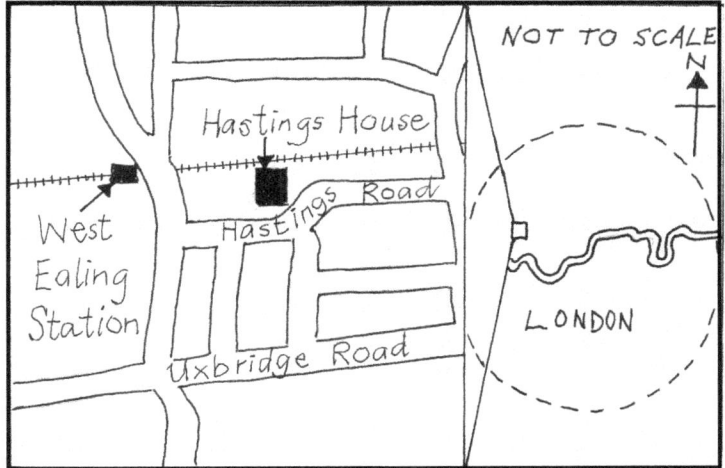

6 West Ealing

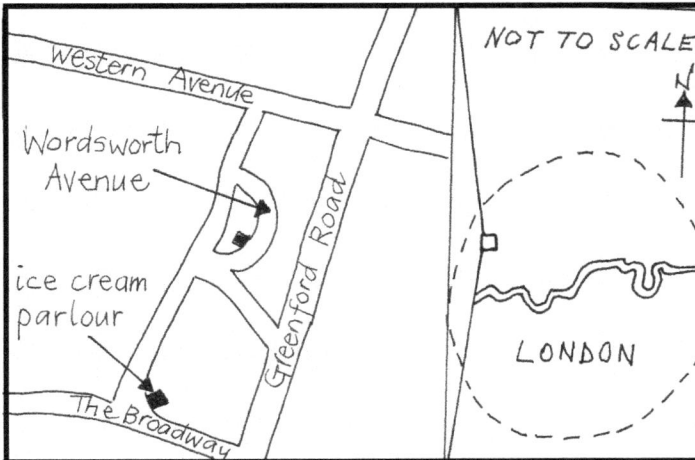

7 Greenford

6 *Talking Books*

My father was a thoughtful and studious man who became interested in some of the new technologies of the twentieth century – for example, motorbikes and radio.

He didn't just work and study for his own sake, however, but had an amiable disposition and took the trouble to help other people on many occasions.

I have a letter (see opposite) which was sent to him from St. Dunstan's, a charity working to help blind servicemen and service-women with an address at Regent's Park.

It's strange to think that forty years later I began to read stories onto audio-tapes, in order to help pupils to improve their reading ability, without realising that my father had helped with the technology of producing talking books for blind people before I had even started at Primary school.

5th May 1941

Dear Mr. Meadows,

Mr. Pinder has told me of the very great interest you have taken in the task of re-equipping the Talking Book Recording Studios after our bombing, and of the very practical help and advice and the valuable introductions you have given him.

It is a matter of very great satisfaction to the National Institute for the Blind and to us, to feel that this Talking Book Library Service to the blind has been able to continue in spite of the bad luck we experienced last autumn, and I write to offer you our very sincere and grateful thanks for the important part you have played in the task of enabling us to get going again. We are most grateful.

Yours sincerely,

Chairman

(to) Standard Telephones and Cables, Ltd., NEW SOUTHGATE, London, N.11.

7 Leicester

A year after the war had ended my father was transferred to a department in Leicester. He worked there from Monday 28th October 1946 until Friday 15th July 1949, at which time he returned to London. Fortunately for me my parents decided not to move northwards but to remain at Whetstone, and so I didn't have to change schools and make new friends.

My father commuted between the two locations, leaving for Leicester on Monday morning and returning home on Friday evening. He made the trip either by train or by motorbike.

He had begun to keep a diary in January 1947 and sometimes made a note of how long his journeys took. For example, on 20th January 1947 he wrote: "To Leicester on Freddie (his Ariel motorbike) 3¼ hours door to door." On Friday 2nd January 1948 he wrote: "Caught 4.16 pm - Home by 7.15 pm." This means that he caught the train to London and then came back to Totteridge and Whetstone underground station where he could take a 251 bus which stopped opposite our flats.

While working at Leicester he stayed at the YMCA (Young Men's Christian Association) hostel and remained active in his spare time.

On Tuesday 25th March 1947 he arranged to start receiving some private coaching in Maths - "am going to have a good go at Maths this time"- and for at least part of his two and a half years there he studied at college.

He had been an enthusiastic photographer in the 1930s and so he became a member of a camera club. On Wednesday 8th October 1947 he wrote: "Session with Miss Barnett and Don Robinson re. camera club." On Tuesday 14th October he noted: "Camera Club in the evening." He entered for at least one exhibition and I still have some of his photos.

He also became interested in using the microscope. On 13th October he bought a book about the microscope and on 28th he bought a collection of 13 slides for 6/6d (£0.32). It's clear that he continued to develop his interest in technical and scientific matters.

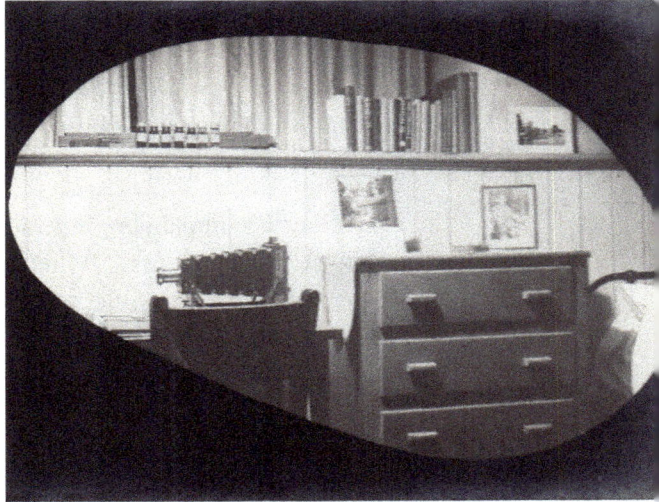

8 *Through the Hole in the Wall*
This was the title of a photograph taken by my father of his room at Leicester.

9 Another Photograph Taken by My Father
He described it as *Theme for an Inn Sign*.

8 Dad's Practical Skills

I have a photo of an aeroplane, taken outside our flat, which reminds me that my father also had a go at making model aircraft. One can almost see from this model how it was constructed. The usual method was to make a light-weight framework out of balsa wood and to paste tissue paper onto it.

The paper was then covered with 'dope' – a liquid substance which helped to strengthen the paper. Finally it was fitted with a small petrol engine and a propeller.

I can remember accompanying my father to Bethune Park, where there was a large expanse of grass, so that he could fly the plane without too much danger of it vanishing over the horizon. Most of the time was spent in trying to make it start, which could cause a certain amount of irritation, but when it did eventually fly it was an impressive sight.

10 A Model Aeroplane

11 My Father with an Engine and Propeller for his Model Aeroplane

12 My Father with Me and his Model Car

Apart from making working models of a locomotive and an aeroplane my father also made a model sports car which he gave me as a present for Christmas or my birthday. He assembled it from a kit, and it seems that he entered this photo for an exhibition in Leicester, for on the back he wrote "Class 1946, Group C." (See Fig. 12 on previous page.)

My father subscribed to such magazines as the *Aeromodeller* and *Model Engineering*, and I still have an image in my mind from one of the magazines of a plump Chinese mandarin with a curving fishing rod reeling in a fish at the end of his line. At that time I was not especially interested in China and, as I can't remember the details, I have no idea what the story had to do with model engineering!

My father was also able to use his practical woodworking skills to help the family. In the cold and snowy February of 1947 he took some time off from working with his lathe in order to make a sledge for me. We tried it out and after that he fitted some metal runners under it so that it would slide more easily over the snow. I can even remember my mother pulling me along on it on our way to school one morning!

A year later, in March 1948, my father designed and made a portable clothes post for mother. It clamped onto the balcony wall next to one of the buttresses and I still have a photo of my mother and Mrs. Wood, our neighbour at number 3, standing next to two lines of washing.

13 The Clothes Line on *Wash Day.*
My mother is facing away from the camera and is talking to a neighbour, Mrs Wood.

Monday Morning

9 My Parents' Health

Although my parents were able to work hard they didn't enjoy the best of health. After the war my mother often suffered from headaches and was occasionally ill with bronchitis or influenza. Her back began to cause her some problems and she was very pleased to begin heat treatment in November 1951, after which her back began to feel better.

She also began to suffer from varicose veins and on Sunday 11th July 1948 she recorded in her diary: "Rested. Leg very bad." Eventually she had to wear special elastic stockings which gave support to her blood vessels. To the best of my knowledge she had always needed to wear glasses because she was short-sighted.

My father also had weak eye-sight and still had a squint from when he was a boy. Like my mother he endured headaches and ailments such as influenza from time to time. Much later in his life he caught shingles which was extremely painful and made his face unrecognisable because it became so swollen.

More distressing, however, was that he suffered a hernia while at Leicester. In his diary the entry for Monday 14th April 1947 reads: "Strained myself while checking station equipment."* He must have tried to move something which was just too heavy for him. Then on Tuesday 15th April he writes: "Dr. Platt 3.00 pm. He says it's hernia." He was forty-one years old. He was admitted to Finchley Memorial Hospital, Homan ward, on Thursday 10th July, and his operation took place on the afternoon of Friday 11th. He had to spend two weeks in hospital and I suppose that it's true to say that he was never quite the same again.

14 The Author and His Parents at the Seaside
We all had medical problems of one kind or another
but at least we looked healthy in these two photos.

10 Cigarettes...

My parents' health was not improved by their addiction to smoking cigarettes. My mother told me that she had started to smoke because of the stresses and strains caused by the war and I can easily believe this. Although they were not in the armed forces you could say that Londoners, and some other city dwellers, were in the front-line for much of the conflict.

After the danger from conventional bombs was over, we were then subjected to the V1 flying bombs. One such bomb landed on Standard's on 23rd August 1944, killing thirty-three people and injuring over four hundred others to a greater or lesser extent. My father could have been killed, and if the angle of the bomb had been slightly different it might have landed on our flats and killed my mother. After that, the German High Command began to send V2 rockets which were far worse because they came from nowhere and caused even more damage and suffering. No wonder that my mother felt the need to benefit from the calming influence of nicotine!

She may also have been influenced by the fact that my father was a heavy smoker. He himself had doubtless been influenced by the tremendous amount of advertising in the 1930s, when so many films, plays and novels showed their characters lighting cigarettes in order to seem suave and debonair. At that time it wasn't clear that cigarettes could damage your health, but my parents learned the hard way. In February 1947 my mother tried to ration her smoking; on Monday 23rd August 1948 she "started a real effort to give up smoking" and on Wednesday 22nd June 1950 "Chas and I decided to give up smoking." They failed to do so. It was because they realised that cigarettes were a kind of drug that they asked me to refrain from starting. "Look what it's done to us!"

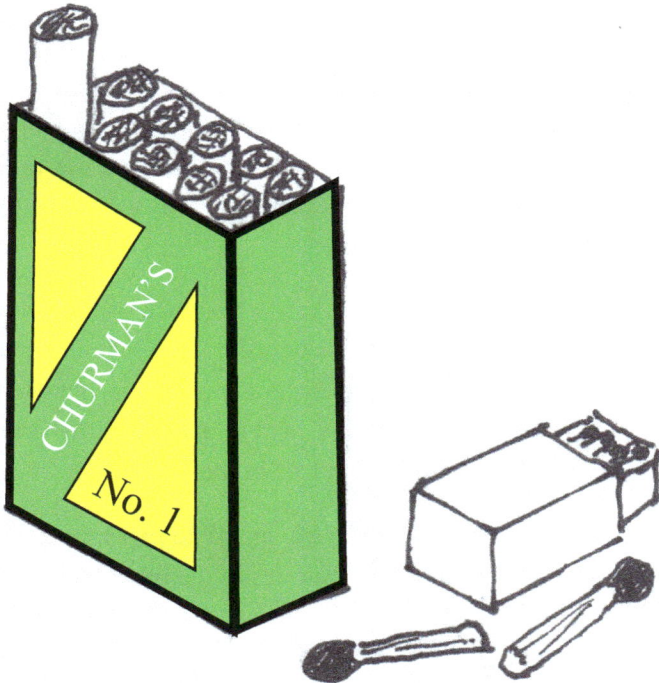

15 Sketch of a Pack of my Father's Favourite Cigarettes, Churchman's No.1, with a box of matches alongside

11 ...and Smoking

I listened to what my parents told me about the perils of smoking, but I still experimented to a small extent, perhaps when I was in my last year or so at primary school, or it may have been during my first year at grammar school.

This was due to 'peer-pressure.' One or two friends began to smoke cigarettes and so I also tried them. At that time the law was more lax than now and some tobacconists would sell individual cigarettes to young people. Fortunately for me I never liked the taste and never bought cigarettes for myself. As a result I only smoked a few times and therefore never became addicted.

I remember that my mother kept a beautiful wooden box which was divided into two sections; in one half she kept the remains of previously smoked cigarettes, which were known as *fag-ends*, but which she called *dog-ends*. She would unroll each dog-end carefully and extract the tobacco, which she kept in that half of the box.

She also kept a packet of *Rizla* cigarette papers, some filters and a gadget for making her own cigarettes in the other half of the box. She would take a *Rizla* paper, put it into her cigarette maker with a filter at one end and stuff tobacco into the rest of the space. After licking along one edge of the paper in order to make it stick, she would twist the gadget so that it produced a cigarette which was as good as one which had been commercially produced.

My father never made his own cigarettes. There were many brands of cigarettes on sale in England in the 1940s, such as *Players*, *Senior Service* and *Woodbines*, but they were all an unhealthy way of burning money! My father's preferred brand was *Churchman's No. 1* (**15**; see previous page**).

16 Mother's tobacco box

12 Chain Smoking

My father was a Civil Servant working for a department of the Ministry of Supply. As such he was probably not highly paid and yet he must have spent a considerable amount of money on cigarettes. He was a 'chain smoker,' which means that there were times when he would light one cigarette after another. I don't remember any of his brothers smoking cigarettes and it's interesting to note that all three of my uncles managed to buy their own houses, whereas after their marriage my parents lived in rented accommodation for the rest of their lives.

I can remember several occasions when my father had to tell me off for doing something wrong. He would summon me to their bedroom, where he had his desk by the window, and I would stand, slowly hopping from one foot to the other, while he told me the story of his life. As he explained the difficulties which he had experienced, perhaps mentioning *From Log Cabin to White House* by an American president, he would light a cigarette.

First of all he opened his cigarette-case, extracted a cigarette, tapped it two or three times on the case to settle the tobacco and then placed it in his mouth. He replaced the case in his pocket, took his cigarette-lighter, flicked it with his thumb so that the flint produced a spark which ignited the wick, and then put the flame to the end of his cigarette. He then continued his speech until the cigarette was finished, whereupon he repeated the ritual.

Of course, in the England of the 21st century he wouldn't be allowed to breathe cigarette smoke all over me for reasons of *Health and Safety*.

17 Burning Money!

It amazes me that so many people are willing to burn some of their money by smoking tobacco.

13 My Health

Time will tell whether or not my parents' smoking had an effect on me. I've never been a particularly strong person physically, but I don't think that 'passive-smoking' stunted my growth. After all, I grew to a height of about 5'10¾ " (five foot ten and three-quarter inches: 1.76 metres?). I suffered from various illnesses as a child but I don't think that I was ever frail.

My chief disadvantage was that, like my parents, I was short-sighted and needed to wear glasses from an early age. I used to attend the optician at Holly Park Clinic, which was only about half a mile (800 metres) from our flat as the crow flies.

Although glasses helped me to see clearly for long distances, having to wear them hindered my activities and they got broken several times while I was growing up. I usually took them off when I wanted to become involved in energetic exercise, but I didn't have a case for them when I was young and so had to put them somewhere safe, which was always a bother.

I also attended the dentist regularly, for a while at the Holly Park Clinic and then at a clinic in Bowes Road, just beyond Arnos Grove Station, next to the swimming pool and library.

I visited Bowes Road on Wednesday 30th June 1948 and received a new *top plate*. This was designed to fit in the top of my mouth in order to space my teeth so that there would be room for new teeth to grow properly rather than being crooked. I was supplied with a tiny key which I used to open the plate a small amount so that it felt very tight in my mouth. My mouth expanded within a few days and I was then able to repeat the process.

18 The Author Wearing NHS Spectacles.
He was still quite young in this photo.. NHS
(National Health Service) spectacles are publicly
funded and quite simple in design.

14 My Mother at Standards

During the war my mother had earned some money by book-keeping, which she was able to do at home. She started working for a firm called *Barrett and Bolton* in February 1943, but this work came to an end on Friday 5th October 1945. On 11th February 1946 she noted in her diary: "Muriel Carminati came with news of a part-time job at Standards," but it wasn't until a year later, on Monday 28th April 1947, that mother started work there.

It was light and relatively easy engineering work, although probably somewhat repetitive, but she had to be there ready for work at 8.30 am. Fortunately the walk took her very little time. She then worked until 1.15 pm, after which she returned home for the rest of the day. She didn't commence full-time working until April 1954, by which time I was seventeen and in the Lower Sixth Form at grammar school. I can't remember when she eventually ceased working at Standards, but I certainly wasn't a poor, deprived *latch-key child.**

It so happened that my parents decided that they could trust me to carry my own key at some time after I had joined St. James's School and I was happy to come home and let myself into the flat if my mother happened to be out. I liked to be alone and to get on with my own activities such as reading, and I never felt disadvantaged. It was unfortunate that I lost this key not long after it had been given to me, and I lost it almost certainly because I had been wrestling on the pavement on my way home. The fact that I had taken so little care of our precious key naturally annoyed my parents.

The next afternoon as I was returning home along Church Crescent I saw a cat sitting majestically in a garden. I stopped to look at it and a woman said to me, "Hallo. Do you know anyone who's lost a key?" On examining it I found that it was mine! As the old saying puts it:

"It's better to be lucky than rich." After that my parents tied the key to a lanyard which I placed around my neck and the key fitted into my right-hand trouser pocket. Since that time I have always kept my keys in my right-hand pocket and I don't remember ever losing them again.

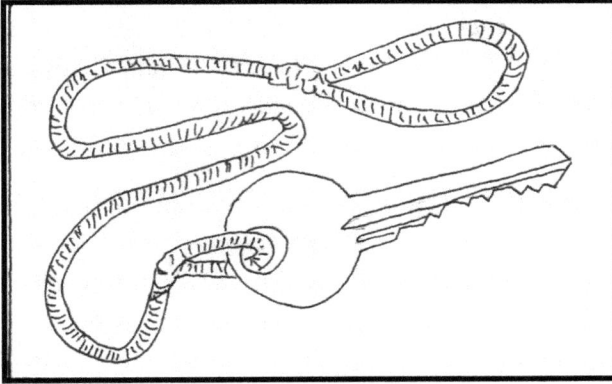

19 My Yale Key on its Lanyard

20 The Cat that Helped Me Recover My Lost Key.

15 Mother's Friends at Standards

My mother benefited by working at Standards, not only because she was able to earn her own money rather than always relying on my father, but also because she was able to meet new people. Two of her special friends were Alice Stevens and Gladys Wilson, both of whom were married. Alice had a daughter called Betty, and I still have a couple of photographs showing mother and me, Alice, Betty and Gladys at Southend while on a coach trip organised by Standards. The five of us went on such an outing to Southend at least twice.

My mother invited both of them to our flat from time to time and also liked to visit them at their homes. Gladys lived at 105 Fountains Crescent, which was a semi-detached house just off Winchmore Hill Road, about two miles (three kilometres) from our flat as the crow flies. I can remember meeting my mother there after school on several occasions. I would walk along Myddleton Park to Oakleigh Road, catch a 125 bus to Southgate Station and then walk down Winchmore Hill Road to her house.

I wasn't bored while they chatted together in the living room because I liked to play at Red Indians! (Of course, it's politically incorrect to use this term in the 21st century; now they are American Indians or members of the First Nations.) I would go upstairs to the toilet and then creep down the stairs on my stomach, through the doorway and behind the sofa without them hearing me. My mother was always annoyed with me whenever I suddenly appeared from behind the sofa, because she thought that I was spying on them, but I wasn't in the least bit interested in what they had to say. All that mattered to me was my game.

21 Mother and Alice at Southend

22 Bernard and Betty

16 A Silly Mistake

I regret to say that as a small boy I didn't always listen to what my mother told me. I often had my head in a book and she would say, "Bernard! Can you empty the rubbish for me?" I would mumble a reply and then ten minutes or half an hour later I would realise that she had said something. There were also times when I wasn't reading but still failed to pay adequate attention.

On one occasion, in the spring or summer of 1948, she told me that she wasn't going to pay her usual weekly visit to Gladys Wilson and therefore I didn't need to go over to Southgate after school. I may have heard what she said, but I didn't take it in, and so of course I made my way over to Gladys's house.

Knock, knock! "Hello, Mrs. Wilson!"

"What are you doing here? Your mummy hasn't come today. Didn't she tell you?"

"Oh dear. I'm sorry to have bothered you."

"Will you be all right?"

"Oh, yes. I expect so. Bye, bye."

I had no idea what to do, because we didn't have a telephone and I had no money for the bus fare home. Of course, mobile phones had still not been invented and wouldn't appear for another half century. I just turned around and began to walk home. It was about 2½ miles (4 kilometres) to our flats by road but it didn't seem to do me any harm. You could say that this was when I started to follow one of my philosophies of life: just put one foot after the other.

Did this help me to pay more attention in future? Perhaps it did, but sometimes I lose concentration when someone says something which starts a train of thought in my mind. Similarly, I sometimes seem rude when I interrupt someone, but this is because I'm very interested in what he or she is saying and this leads me to a new train of thought with the result that I respond too quickly.

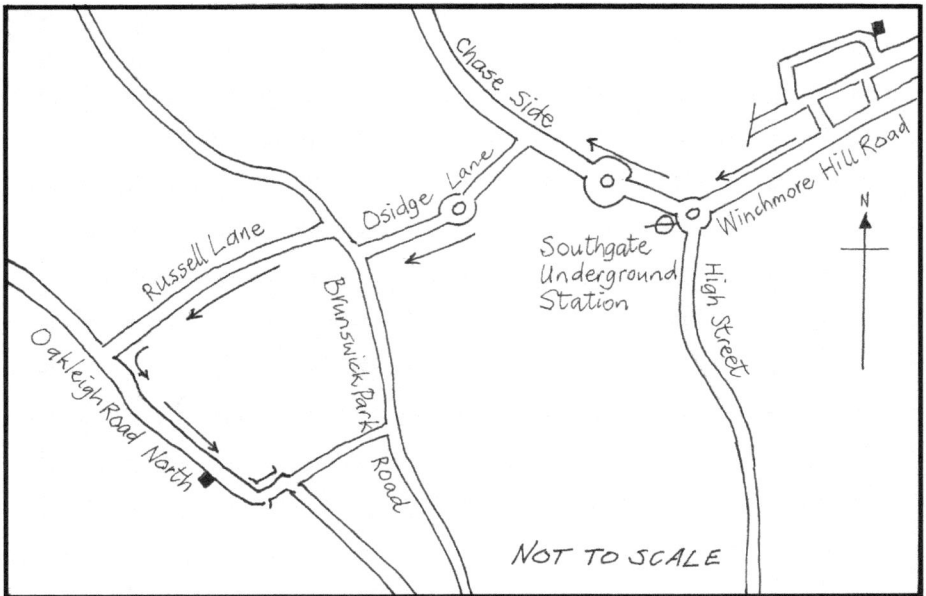

23 My Route Home

17 My Chores

I believe that it's true to say that I was always a friendly and helpful child. However, I enjoyed reading so much and buried my head in a book so often that I wasn't always willing to get on and do practical household jobs. On the other hand I was always happy to receive my pocket money!

There was only one chore which I didn't like and that was cleaning the brass. My parents had two brass fire irons – a long poker (for poking the fire) and a long pair of tongs (for picking up lumps of coal). I was expected to clean their brass handles, and also a couple of brass ornaments, by rubbing them with a special cloth on which I had tipped some liquid *Brasso*. I didn't like this at all. I was much happier doing the washing up, i.e. washing our crockery and cutlery in the sink, and was equally happy to use a drying-up cloth to dry the plates and dishes, and the knives, forks and spoons.

When I could tear myself away from a book I was very happy to run errands for my mother. From an early age I became used to going to *The Pantry* to buy our loaves of bread, which were invariably *split tins* and to the butcher to collect the meat for our Sunday lunch, which was usually a piece of *topside* (**25**). Every Saturday I walked up the hill to Barfields, our local newsagents, in order to pay our newspaper bill.

Sometimes I went around the corner to the post office to buy stamps or to post a letter, and I often went to the greengrocer's and the grocer's, which were next to each other on the opposite side of the road.

Before I left junior school I was able to look at my mother's shopping list upside-down, while the grocer was adding up the cost of the items, and then work out the answer before he did. This was necessary because he sometimes made mistakes, and they were always in his favour, never in ours!

24 Barfield's Newsagents

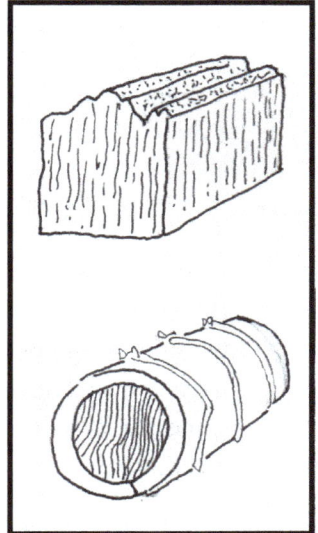

25 A Split Tin (top) and a Piece of Topside

26 Oakleigh Road Post Office

This is now a family home.

18 London Zoo

My mother's diary for Monday 8th September 1947 has the entry: "Zoo! Gladys, Muriel and Bernard." This refers to London Zoo, which is situated in the north-east corner of Regent's Park. According to my encyclopaedia: "The first authenticated zoological garden was that of a Chinese emperor in 1100 B.C.," but London Zoo only dates back to 1826.

I seem to remember that we travelled as far as Camden Town on the Northern Line and then walked to the entrance. Once inside the zoo we were faced with various signposts which pointed us in every direction. I'm sure that we went to see the giraffes, polar bears, brown bears and then the penguins and seals, but the lions were especially impressive pacing up and down in their cages. We visited the Elephant House, saw some adults and children having elephant- and camel-rides, and also went into the Reptile House, the Insect House and the Aquarium.

All the creatures in the zoo lived in cramped conditions compared with their lives in the wild, but presumably the living conditions were most restrictive for the mammals. Efforts were made later after the war to improve the amount of space available, but it is surely impossible to recreate the natural conditions which are found in the wild.

Whipsnade Zoo, which is situated about thirty-five miles to the north-west of Central London, has very large paddocks available for many different mammals, but it still has fences around it and so it, too, is really a prison for animals. I suppose that it will always be difficult to reconcile the conflicting views of those who want to abolish zoos and those who want to keep them for purposes of research and conservation.

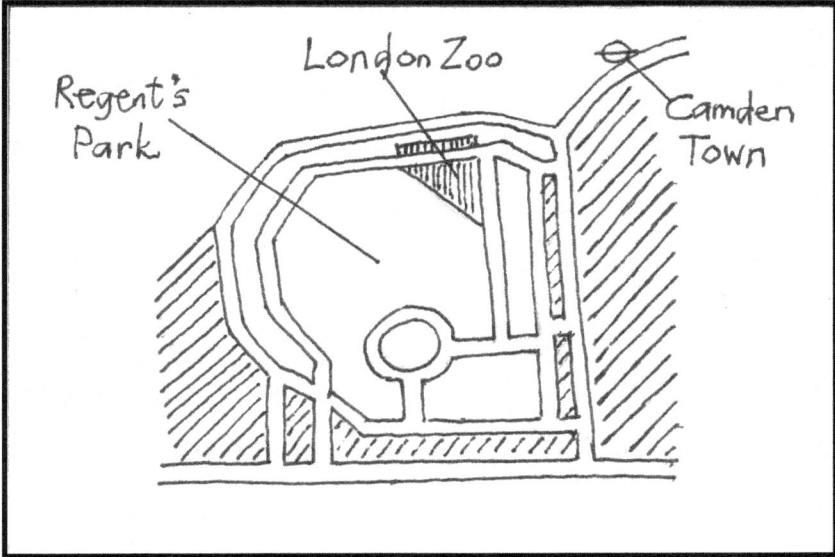

27 London Zoo

19 The Circus

I believe that I have only ever been to one circus and that was on Thursday 15th January 1948. My mother had to attend a Parents' Evening at St. James's School and so Gladys Wilson took me, perhaps because she didn't have any children of her own.

We travelled into town by tube as far as Olympia where there was a huge stadium, for it was here that the Bertram Mills Circus held its performances. I can't remember the exact details of that night's performance but on Friday 16th January my father wrote in his diary: "Home on the 5.17, arrived by 8.20 pm. Es [Esme] busy with new curtains and Bernard very full of a visit to Bertram Mills Circus."

I was eager to talk about my experiences because there had been lots of bright lights, music which was sometimes jolly and sometimes dramatic, and plenty of non-stop activity. The clowns were always energetic and occasionally even amusing. I'm not sure that I found their slapstick comedy very funny even at the age of eleven.

I was far more impressed by the trapeze artists who risked their lives by flying through the air from one trapeze to another and the tightrope walkers (high wire artistes), balancing themselves with long poles, who were part of that act. I admired anyone who showed physical skills, such as the equestrian riders who jumped on and off their horses and performed balancing tricks on their horses' backs.

I was also impressed by the lion-tamers—or were they showing their dominance over tigers? In any case, animal acts are no longer in fashion; they are another activity which is frowned upon as being 'politically incorrect' in England in the 21st century. I remember that a couple of my school friends and I were so impressed with what we had seen that we spent an hour or two playing at 'circuses.'

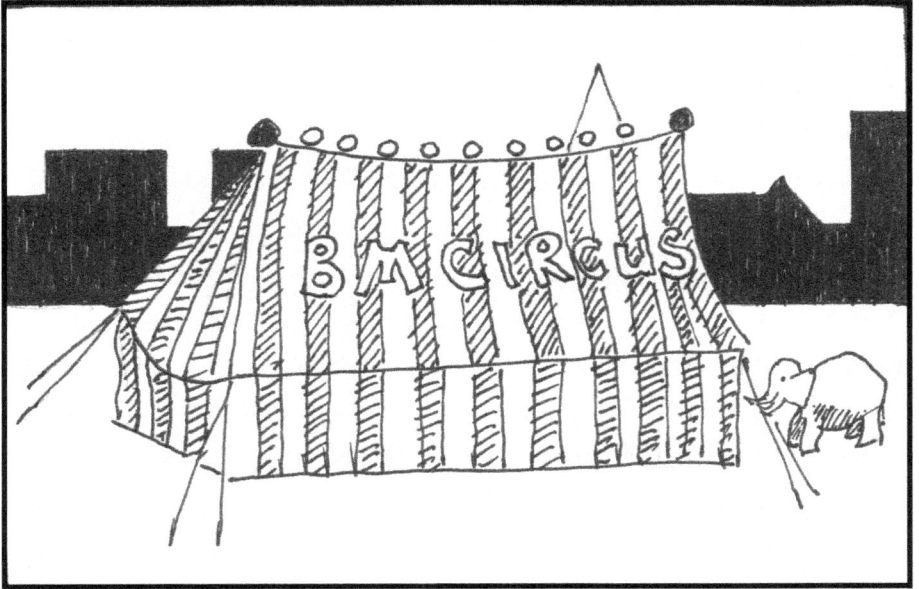

28 A 'Big Top' Circus Tent

20 Christmas 1947

Christmas and Easter are the two most important Christian festivals in England. Although belief in Christianity has declined considerably in England during the past hundred years, these two festivals are still an important part of our cultural tradition.

I consider the New Year celebrations to be part of Christmas, as they are only a week apart, and for many people they are part of the same holiday. The Christmas and New Year period is generally considered to be the time of year when families try to be reunited, but in 1947 we stayed at home rather than visiting relatives.

My mother put up Christmas decorations which consisted of Christmas cards which had been sent to us and coloured paper chains which she and I had made ourselves. We hung the paper chain across our living room from one corner to another. Mother also bought a small Christmas tree on which we fitted glass balls and other ornaments.

Each year, on Christmas morning (December 25th), I found a large stocking filled with presents next to my bed, which always filled me with excitement. The only present which I remember from 1947 was a stamp album from my father. In May of that year he had bought me a book about philately and for a while I was keen to collect postage stamps which were both aesthetically pleasing and of geographical interest. I wasn't interested in valuable stamps which were rare but unattractive; I wanted to produce pleasing patterns on the pages of my album.

For our Christmas dinner my mother usually served us with roast turkey together with Brussels sprouts, roast potatoes, carrots and roasted parsnips. After this we enjoyed mince pies, which I had helped to make, and Christmas pudding with custard, which was very rich and filling. After that my father often felt like taking a nap! That Christmas we went over the road to Mrs. Carminati for tea and took the opportunity to look at their television, which was still a rarity at that time.

29 A Christmas Tree with Ornaments

30 A Christmas Stocking

31 A Christmas Meal

Chapter 4

1948

List of Memories

1 The New Year and Easter 1948

I still have in my possession a cow horn which came from my mother's side of the family. It seems that she continued an old custom. Each year, on 31st December, she and I would go onto the balcony and blow the horn as the clock on the radio began to strike midnight. Each of us blew it just once, and it took so much breath that the two of us finished blowing before the clock had struck twelve. In this way we blew out the old year and blew in the new. The horn made a raucous sound and I must admit that I have discontinued this custom. Perhaps it should be revived!

I've long felt that the first two or three months of the year are an anticlimax to the Christmas period, as the weather in England is usually cold and miserable, but as Shelley puts it: *"If winter's here, can spring be far behind?"* As a boy I could always look forward to Easter*, not only because the weather was likely to be better, but because it was the custom to give children a chocolate Easter egg. On Good Friday, 26.3.1948, I recorded in my very first diary: "I had an Easter egg."

Some people in Europe like to paint eggs at this time, because eggs represent new life and spring is the time when many plants and animals reproduce. A few people used to like to use a needle or pin to make a tiny hole in an egg so that they could suck out the contents. The egg was then much lighter and could be kept for a long time without going bad. That's why the expression: *"Teach your granny to suck eggs"* means that you're telling someone something that he or she knows already. However, in the 20th Century many people decided that it was wrong to go collecting birds' eggs and so this old custom seems to have died out in England.

Something else which I looked forward to was Shrove Tuesday*, which was a few weeks before Easter. My mother made pancakes for our tea by frying batter in a large frying pan and the first time her diary mentioned this was on 10.2.1948.

2 Painted Eggs
Such eggs can be very beautiful but, when I was young, I appreciated chocolate Easter eggs more than the painted ones.

1 Our Cow's Horn
This horn comes from Somerset, or somewhere in the West country. At the narrow end it has a mouth-piece with a reed which enables it to be blown, but it is difficult to make it 'speak.' That is why we couldn't blow it for very long and why it sounded so loud when we blew it.

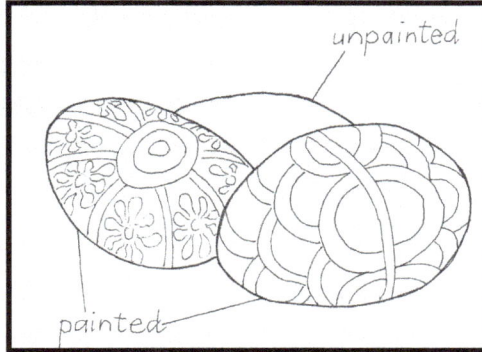

3 Pancakes They can be used as a savoury dish, with a filling of meat or cheese, or they can provide a dessert if filled with fruit or some other sweet substance.

She mixed milk, flour and an egg in a large bowl in order to make the batter. She heated some butter in a frying-pan and then poured a ladle full of batter into the pan so that it cooked quickly. She then flipped it over and cooked the other side so that it became a thin, crispy pancake. She lifted it out and placed it on a piece of greaseproof paper. She sprinkled it with sugar and squeezed some drops of fresh lemon juice onto it, after which she rolled it up. Sometimes she let me sprinkle the sugar and squeeze the lemon juice, and I always enjoyed taking part in the process. They were always delicious and we had them on Shrove Tuesday every year for many years afterwards.

2 An Unfortunate Escapade

"Someone's in yer garden, pickin' all yer flowers." This is what London urchins used to chant in order to embarrass one of their number who was on someone else's property and was therefore trespassing. One afternoon in the week commencing Monday 19th January 1948, when I was just over eleven years old, I was returning home from school along Church Crescent when I was foolish enough to go into one of the gardens with several friends, who probably included John Browne. I don't know why we did this but I do know that an irate man rushed out of his front door and my friends ran away.

4 Someone's in Your Yarden
This piece of music gives an impression of what was chanted in 1948. I wonder if some children had been influenced by the traditional songs and chants of London tradesmen and street-sellers.

Perhaps I was too proud to run. In any case, not only was I stupid enough to let him catch me, but I was also stupid enough to give him my correct name and address when he asked for it. I suppose that I was a little bit like George Washington was reputed to be: *I couldn't bring myself to tell a lie.* Throughout my life I have been disinclined to tell lies, one reason being that I think that they ultimately cause more trouble than telling the truth. Being tactful is, of course, another matter!

I then forgot about the matter except that at the back of my mind I felt somewhat worried. I was in bed on the following Saturday morning when the post arrived and a few minutes later I heard the low murmur of my parents' voices. *"Your father wants to see you,"* said my mother and I went into their bedroom in fear and trembling. I didn't know that my father had by then agreed not to beat me. Instead I had to listen for what seemed like a very long time while my father sat at his desk chain smoking and expressed his displeasure at the complaints made against me by a Mr. L.R. Lewis. It's not surprising that I tried to keep out of trouble as I was growing up!

5 The Author in 1948, aged 11
At this time I had no idea of
how my life would develop.

6 John Browne in 1948
He was my classmate and best
friend from about 1946 onwards.
We kept in contact until he died on
3rd December 2012 at the age of
75. The *Postcript* gives a story of
his life.

139

3 The Hollies

When I was alone I rarely did anything that was anti-social. I was brought up to respect other people and their property and I listened to my conscience which was always a good guide. When I was with friends, however, I was subjected to the same sort of peer-pressure which exists today. As the Germans say: *"Gegen den Strom ist schwer schwimmen"* - *"It's difficult to swim against the stream."*

As I've grown older I've become more scrupulous and conscientious, but I still sometimes find it easier to go along with what other people want even though it's contrary to my moral viewpoint. I suppose that it's part of being sociable, but it's the reason why mobs and mass hysteria can be dangerous and that's why I usually avoid crowds.

I remember that when I was in my last year or so at St. James's Junior School a couple of friends and I trespassed on a property known as *The Hollies*, which was situated on the edge of Whetstone at the top of Oakleigh Road. We went there twice. The site is now covered with a block of flats, which must have been built in about 1950, but when we went there in about 1947 or 1948 it consisted of a large, old and deserted house standing in an extensive garden.

It was exciting for us to creep up and down the staircases and to play hide-and-seek in the rooms. I was encouraged to climb out onto a balcony where there was a wasps' nest, whereupon someone poked the nest with a stick, which also provided an entertaining ten minutes! We threw a number of stones at the windows, but at that time it never entered my head that we might be causing someone's property to decline in value. On our second visit we were surprised to see the blue-clad figure of a policeman come round the corner of the house. We ran away as quickly as we could and I never returned.

7 The Hollies
This is a modern photo from 2009. It
shows the blocks of flats which were
built on the site of the old, derelict house.

4 My Father and Film-making

As I mentioned in a previous memory, my father used a ciné camera before the war to make some short films. On Sunday 1st February 1948, having decided to sell his lathe, he wrote: "I've decided to go back to sub-standard ciné as a hobby." By sub-standard he meant 9.5mm ciné film, which had been popular with amateurs in the pre-war period. The commercial films shown in cinemas usually used strips of film which were 35mm wide, while documentary films tended to use 16mm film.

My father was able to buy 9.5mm film, but 8mm film became much more popular among amateurs in the years after the war. By the end of the 20th century, however, videotape recorders had superseded film cameras because they were easier to use.

On Sunday 8th February my father wrote: "...Looked out 9.5mm films and gear. Found some very old Geveart film and decided to give it a chance." Then on Saturday 14th February he wrote: "Took Bernard over to Camera Craft at Palmers Green to purchase a screen , £1.17.0, (£1.85): film show in the evening!" On Saturday 21st February he collected a short Charlie Chaplin film entitled "Gypsy Life" from Camera Craft, and the next day gave a little film show to our neighbours, Mr. and Mrs. Wood.

On Saturday 27th March my parents and I went down to Pitsea by train. They later returned home and I stayed with my grandparents for the first week of my Easter Holiday. I remember going to Bowers Gifford Church on Easter Sunday, where Granddad was a sidesman*, and feeling faint because of the incense!* At the end of the week, on Saturday 3rd April 1948, my uncle Dave brought my parents, together with my father's film equipment, down to Pitsea in his van so that we could see a film show in the evening. It lasted for about two hours. After that my father's enthusiasm for film-making lasted for several years.

5 My Father and Amateur Radio

My father made a crystal radio set when he was young.   Radio transmissions and related technologies then became an important part of his life both for work and for play. It's not surprising, therefore, that he later became a *radio ham*, i.e. an amateur radio operator licensed by the government to transmit radio messages 'over the air.' The first reference to this that I can find is from his 1948 diary entries for the Whitsun weekend.   This Christian festival commemorates the alleged descent of God's holy spirit to Christ's disciples fifty days after Easter.   On Sunday 16th May my father wrote: "Carrying on with S/Het portable," and on Whit Monday he noted: "More on S/Het portable."   'Superhet' is short for super heterodyne which refers to a special treatment of radio signals.   Then on Saturday 12th June he bought a Morse key buzzer so that he could practise sending messages in Morse code. He wanted to use his voice to communicate with other hams, but the government made it a condition for being granted a licence that all amateurs should also be able to understand and transmit messages in Morse code. This might have been so that they could understand May Day* messages from ships in distress.

On Saturday 24th July 1948 my father wrote: "P.J.R. (probably Mr. Ridgewell) came round and we erected the 134 ft. aerial; our dear friends (my father was being sarcastic) immediately started beefing but having agreed the business with H.K.N (Mr. Nixon) they may beef* as much as they like."   Unlike some of our neighbours I didn't complain, but from that time onwards I often woke up in the morning and then heard my father's voice as he broadcast unimportant gossip to other radio enthusiasts because there were restrictions on what radio hams could say to each other over the air. He reached various parts of England and even some distant locations around the world. I didn't escape this form of reveille until I finally left home in 1965, and he continued with this hobby until not long before his death in 1976.

6 *Golfing and Model-making*

My father clearly had a great influence on me as I was growing up, but I didn't necessarily follow in his footsteps. For example, when he felt the urge to get out his golf clubs again, we went down to the nine-hole golf course* at Bethune Park on Saturday 13th March 1948 and also on the following Saturday. We had first been there together in April 1944, when I was only seven, but I didn't find it any more exciting when I was eleven than I had done at seven and so I didn't bother to develop my skills in this direction. Golf seems to require a great deal of study and practice* in order to achieve satisfying results, but can be very frustrating.

Similarly, I wasn't keen on model-making unless it could be done fairly quickly. At one time my father encouraged me to make a model fighter-plane but I became bored with sandpapering two blocks of wood into the shapes of jet engines and I didn't finish it. On the other hand, I did enjoy using scissors with paper or cardboard.

During the last weekend of February 1948 I made a glider. I had to cut the fuselage, wings and tail from a sheet of printed cardboard and then fit the parts together by pushing the wings and tail through two slots in the fuselage. Afterwards I enjoyed making it glide through the air.

Over sixty-five years later, Ann Brooker, another member of the *Finchley Art Society*, reminded me of a detail which I had forgotten. Some of these model gliders had a nick in the fuselage so that we could attach an elastic band to it (popularly known as a rubber band). We made a catapult with two fingers of one hand, held the tail end of the glider with the other hand and pulled back on the rubber band. When we let go of the glider the force exerted by the rubber band launched the glider into the air.

8 My Father Practising Golf
My father was a keen golfer before World War II, and here he is practising his golf-swing at Hastings House. This photo must date from 1936 or 1937.

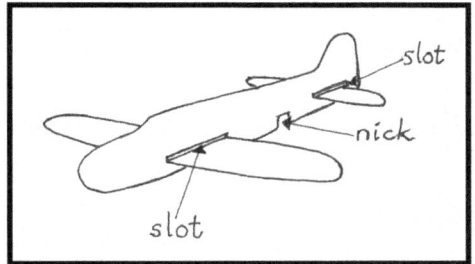

9 A Model Glider
Making a glider like this was my sort of practical activity because it was fairly simple to put the parts **together.**

I also seem to remember making a toy aeroplane for which I only had to assemble some simple parts by using a kit. I believe that the fuselage and wings were made of balsa wood which is very light. It had a plastic propeller which I attached to the nose of the plane. There was some way in which I fitted a rubber band to it, but I can't remember the details. When the rubber band was wound up it provided enough energy to turn the propeller and so made the plane fly for a short distance through the air. These projects were relatively easy for me and were therefore my kind of model-making!

7 The Eleven-plus Examinations

In the spring of 1948 I sat the Scholarship Examinations which were to decide whether or not I could attend a grammar school rather than a secondary modern. My father was keen that I should have the advantage of an academic education because he had not benefited from such an education even though he was a studious man. All his life he tried to make up for what he viewed as a deficiency in his education by continuing to study in various ways.

On Wednesday 24th September 1947 he wrote: "Went up to town to try to get French text-book for Joe Wood (our next-door neighbour) – no luck but got Intelligence Tests for Bernard, also Scholarship papers."*

I can still remember that I practised answering sample intelligence tests several times in the autumn of 1947 and I enjoyed them because they involved attempting to solve puzzles. I also vaguely remember answering questions to test my knowledge of the English language and Arithmetic.

On Tuesday 10th February I took my Preliminary Exams and my results were 40/50, 93/100 and 39/50. The first Scholarship Examination took place on Thursday 26th February and consisted of English and Arithmetic Papers and on Friday 27th I sat the Intelligence Paper. After that I more or less forgot about them, although my father had noted previously on Friday 6th February: "Bernard apparently worrying about his 'special place' exam."

Then later in the summer, on Friday 25th June 1948 he wrote: "Home with Wells. Home by 8.45. Bernard back from camp and very pleased with life – he has passed OK on the scholarship and will be going to Woodhouse." We were fortunate that we lived in an area which was well supplied with grammar schools, but I felt especially fortunate to be going to a school with a good reputation. I could hardly wait for September and the start of a new term and a new school!

10 Woodhouse School
This photo from 2009 shows the front of the building which
became a Sixth Form college some years after I had left it.

8 The Radio

Radio was an important part of my life until I was eighteen, but after that it declined in importance, partly because of the influence of television. When I was young, however, my mother and I often listened to the Home Service and the Light Programme. At that time the Third Programme was too heavy for me because it featured classical music and I preferred lighter and more popular musical entertainment. However, a great deal of light classical music was used as incidental music to radio programmes and so I absorbed such music without realising it.

On Monday 2nd February I wrote in my diary: "Hurried home to listen to Children's Hour." This took place every weekday afternoon and was introduced by 'Uncle Mac' (David Davies) who ended each session with the memorable words "Good night, children, everywhere." There were sometimes adventure serials and I remember that the film stars Naunton Wayne and Basil Radford took part in one of them; they were quietly humorous actors. I remember that there were the boy detectives, Norman and Henry Bones, and *The Green Dolphin Mystery* was the title of another adventure but I can't remember anything else about it.

11 Swallows and Amazons
Arthur Ransome drew his own pictures for his series of books. They were simple sketches, but not as simple as mine!

148

On one occasion I heard an episode from the radio adaptation of *Swallows and Amazons*, a year or so before I began to read the series of books by Arthur Ransome, of which this was the first.

I was somewhat surprised by the name of one of the girls – Titty – but enjoyed hearing about their adventures which involved camping and messing about in boats.

12 Just William
He and his three friends loved to play games in the countryside, but he was always getting into trouble and it was never his fault!

I also enjoyed hearing stories by Richmal Crompton about a boy called William. Her ability to understand how boys think was surprising. Her first book, *Just William*, was published in 1922 and this was followed by over thirty books which included several hundred amusing short stories. William's group of close friends were Douglas, Henry and Ginger and they called themselves *The Outlaws*. Their mission was to *Right Wrongs* which usually entailed exposing the hypocrisies and conceits of grownups. Great stuff. William was a kind of modern day Robin Hood.

It would seem that the radio was able to reinforce my interest in reading and also gave me access to beautiful music. *"Thank you, the British Broadcasting Corporation!"*

9 Dramatic Entertainment

Because I attended elocution lessons for about three years from the age of eight, I became acquainted with some of the processes involved in acting. Perhaps we practised mime with Miss Stanley because some of the pupils were considered to be potential actors and actresses, and of course it is important for such entertainers to speak clearly. While I was young my experience of the theatre was limited to popular productions such as pantomimes and musicals.

On 2nd January 1946 my mother and I went to the Wood Green Empire to see Jack and Jill – a pantomime based on the old nursery rhyme:

Jack and Jill went up the hill
To fetch a pail of water,
Jack fell down and broke his crown
And Jill came tumbling after.

I can't remember anything about it, but I expect that the plot was based on the poem. There would have been several songs and dance routines, beautiful costumes together with attractive scenery and lighting, topical jokes and slapstick comedy, and a happy ending.

On Wednesday 3rd September 1947 my mother took Auntie May and me to see *Annie Get Your Gun*, a musical about an American cowgirl who was a sharpshooter, and on Tuesday 20th January 1948 my mother, Gladys Wilson and I went to see *Peter Pan*, a pantomime based on the book by Sir James Barrie.*

This was a fantasy story which involved young children flying through the air to *Neverland* and included fairies, pirates and Red Indians. Peter Pan was a boy who had never grown up. He lived in *Neverland* and had fairies as his friends, but he had a great enemy, Captain Hook, so-called because he had a hook in place of one his hands which had been bitten off by a crocodile. In the pantomime Captain Hook managed to poison a fairy called Tinkerbell and I can still remember all of us children clapping our hands in order to save her life. Peter Pan called out to the children: "Do you believe in fairies?" At that time, I probably did.

12 Jack and Jill
Many of our nursery rhymes have political or social comments hidden within them, but I don't know if this one has any special significance.

10 Sweets and Ice Cream

When I was young, I had a sweet tooth. Nowadays I believe that too many sweets can endanger our health, but my mother used to like chocolate and so I also came to enjoy it. Her favourite chocolate bar was Cadbury's Fruit and Nut, which consisted of raisins and hazelnuts in milk chocolate. It's possible that she thought that the nutritious fruit and nuts would counteract the dangers of eating the chocolate. Be that as it may, I was brought up to enjoy sweets, and I particularly liked liquorice allsorts. These consisted of pieces of liquorice with different shapes which were often combined with a form of 'icing.'

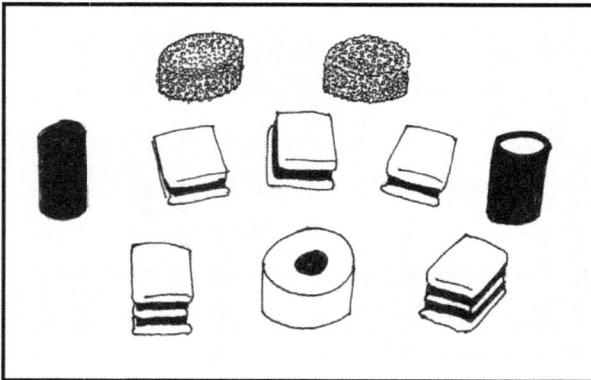

14 Liquorice Allsorts
These had a high sugar content and were therefore not at all healthy, but they are still very tasty in the 21st century!

I also enjoyed ice-cream in its various forms. When I went to the kiosk in the park near my grandfather's home at Pitsea, I either bought a wafer or an ice cream cornet.

The 'wafer' consisted of two rectangular, biscuit-like wafers with vanilla ice cream in between them. Some shops provided firm ice cream which came wrapped in paper, but other shops put soft ice cream in the wafers by using a metal gadget which was filled with ice-cream; a wafer biscuit was then placed on the two sides of the slab. The kiosk in the park gave me soft ice cream so that I had to lick my wafer quickly before the ice cream melted. If I bought a cornet, the person behind the

15 An Ice-cream Cornet and a Choc-ice
The cornet held a pre-formed slab of ice-cream which had been wrapped in paper until it was put into the cornet. It was not as exciting, or as delicious, as the Italian ice-cream which came from the nozzle of a machine. The choc ice was a slab of ice-cream covered in a thin layer of chocolate and held in its wrapper in order to eat it.

counter would take a short, cylindrical piece of hard ice cream, un-wrap the paper which surrounded its sides and push it firmly into the top of the cornet-shaped biscuit container. This usually melted slowly.

This was very different from so-called Italian ice cream which was like a very thick cream and usually came from a machine. The cornet was placed against a nozzle on the machine and this gave it a shape as it was squeezed onto the cornet. Some shops used a scoop to make balls of ice cream which could be placed onto a cornet or into a bowl.

My favourite ice cream, however, was undoubtedly the choc ice. This was a bar of firm vanilla-flavoured ice cream which was covered in chocolate. I believe that we could buy milk-chocolate coated bars, but I preferred dark choc ices. For several years after the Second World War I used to watch out for an ice cream man who rode his tricycle down Oakleigh Road, and I believe that his choc ices used to cost 3d each (5p). He had a large box in front of him which was part of the bike and which contained a variety of ices. Like all his colleagues he had a slogan on the front of the box: "*Stop me – and buy one.*" I was always happy to do so – when I had the money!

11 Jigsaw Puzzles

When I was young I sometimes played with jigsaw puzzles. Most of the commercial puzzles were made of cardboard, but good quality puzzles were made of wood. In order to cut wood into pieces it is necessary to use a fretsaw or a jigsaw. That is why they are called jigsaw puzzles.

Long ago someone gave my father five home-made jigsaw puzzles which were stored in five large cigarette boxes, and I still have them hidden away in a cupboard.

At one time I had a wooden jigsaw puzzle which featured Peter Pan. It showed a number of trees in a forest. Some of the trees had doors in their trunks, and the cutaway parts of the picture* showed Peter Pan and the children sleeping in rooms in the ground underneath the trees. Above ground were some pirates, led by Captain Hook, and they were creeping up to the doors. Unfortunately I no longer have what was an attractive little jigsaw puzzle.

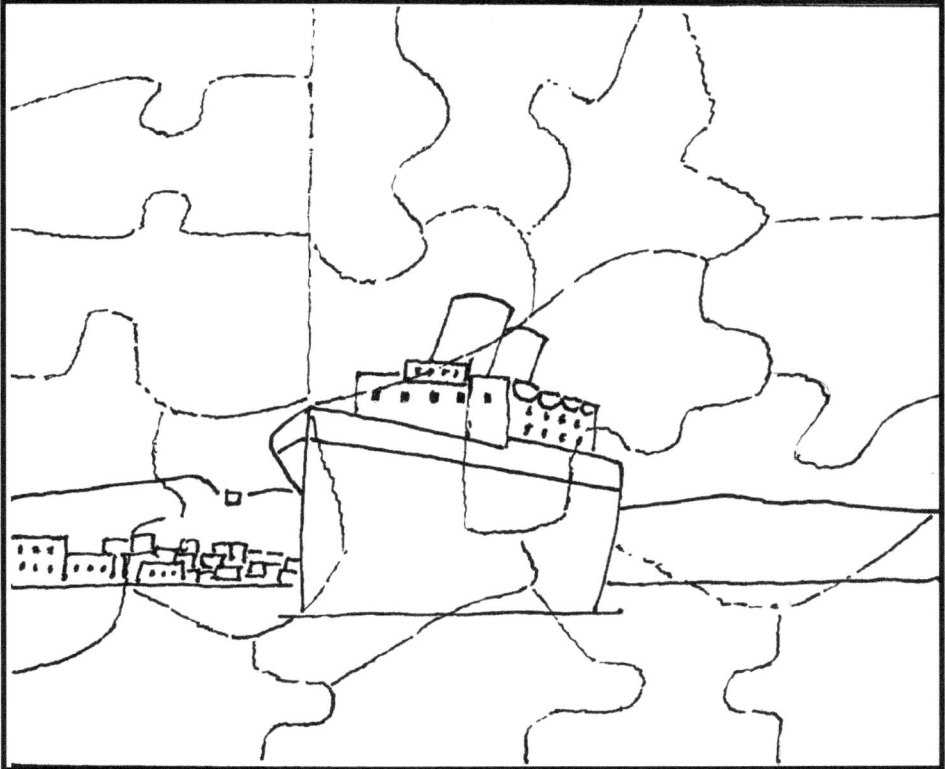

16 A Jig-saw Puzzle

This is my version of a hand-made wooden puzzle constructed by one of my father's friends before the Second World War. It shows the *Steamship Cantara in Vigo Bay*. The little picture was stuck onto plywood and then cut into intricate pieces with a jig-saw. My puzzle looks easy because it has only eighteen pieces whereas the original has 104.

12 My Acting Ability

Although my elocution lessons helped me to improve my speech and my ability to act silently, I was never keen on acting as such. Nor did I enjoy dressing up in a theatrical way. I can remember only two occasions when I was involved in dramatic activities while at St. James's, and they weren't school productions but were part of our class activities.

On one occasion I played the part of Robin Hood in a little play that Miss Leroy produced for our class. I seem to remember that my mother dyed* a shirt green for me because Robin was said to have lived in the greenwood and, therefore, he and his men wore green clothing. I had a wooden sword about two feet long, which my father had made for me, and we fitted our cow-horn with a strap so that I could hang it from my neck and under my right arm. Apart from these details I can remember nothing of the play, but I still have the horn and keep it lying on the chest of drawers in our living room.

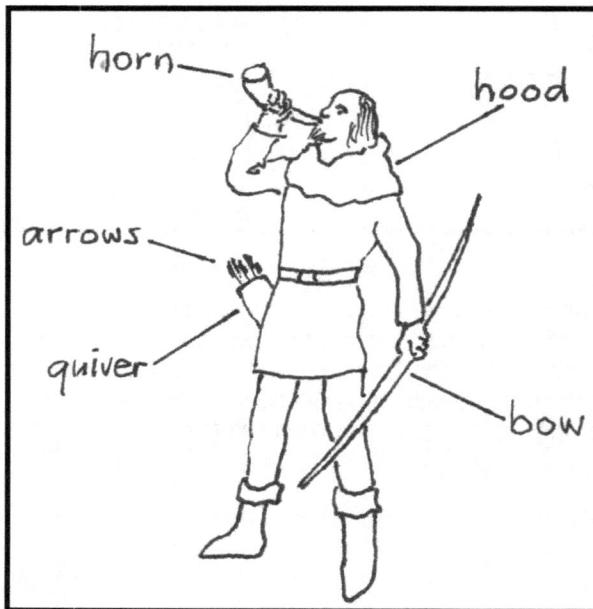

17 Robin Hood
This famous legend tells us that Robin used to blow his horn in order to summon his band of outlaws together before they went off on their adventures. It was the Anglo-Saxon response to the fact that the country had been successfully invaded by the Normans in 1066.

18 A Bowl of Fruit
Each piece of fruit
was given a human
personality in our
little school play.

The other occasion was when Miss Leroy's class acted out a little play, published for schools, which featured a bowl of fruit. I believe that I was the banana and there were also an apple, an orange, a pear and a plum in the bowl*. Naturally we were able to talk and we discussed the family that we were 'living' with. I was so busy trying to remember my line, that I was only dimly aware of the main ideas of the play! My line was, "*They've all gone into the dining room and shut the door.*" We rehearsed it several times and probably performed it for the parents but I can't be sure about that.

Later in life I appeared in several school productions, both as a pupil and when I was a teacher, but always in minor roles. Usually I preferred to work behind the scenes because I'm not a natural actor.

13 The Cinema

As I mentioned earlier the cinema played an important part in my life as I was growing up, but I sometimes had to wait in a long queue to get in. Some queues stretched around the block because the cinema was such a popular form of entertainment. Each cinema would open in the early afternoon and offer two feature films, some adverts, and trailers for films which were coming shortly. The programme was repeated almost continually until the late evening with an interval between the A and B films.

Each cinema gave an impression of luxury and the *Gaumont*, Finchley, had an electric organ placed in front of the screen. As the lights went up for the interval between the two films the organ would rise majestically from a pit with the organist playing popular music, but I must say that I didn't like the sound of the cinema organ very much because of its tone colour. The large, electric cinema organ was powerful, but to my ears it sounded very heavy and "dead."

Once or twice I attended the special children's Saturday morning performances. These often included a cowboy serial in which the hero was in an impossible situation at the end of one episode, but was able to escape at the beginning of the next one a week later!

I sometimes went to the pictures alone or with a couple of school friends, but I often went with my mother. I enjoyed *The Four Feathers*, an adventure story which was produced in 1939 and was one of the early colour films. It was set in 1885 and its hero went to Egypt and the Sudan as a spy during a British war in the 19th century because he had been accused of being a coward.*

Green for Danger was a murder mystery with the comic actor Alastair Sim as a police inspector; it was produced in 1946 and I must have seen it when I was about ten or eleven years old. I can still remember my shock when the doors of the hospital operating theatre blew open in the wind to reveal a white-clad figure – the murderer!

On Thursday 1st January 1948 my mother and I went to see *It Always Rains on Sunday*, with the blonde actress Googie Withers, in which a man was convicted of a murder which he hadn't committed. As I grew up my visits to the cinema increased my knowledge of the world around me and so were not merely a form of entertainment. Films provided me with another source of information beyond that which I obtained from books and the radio.

19 A Cinema Organ
In some cinemas this provided further entertainment between the two main films. The organist played a variety of music which would include some popular pieces of the time.

14 "The past is another country!"

In 1948 my parents and I were actually living in the post-war period, but it felt as though we were still part of the pre-war culture. It may be that, when peace has been declared, people instinctively try to revert to the way of life that they were used to before the war. Warfare, however, may bring about social changes and technological advances so that it acts as a watershed and within a few years a society's culture may change considerably.

In 1948 the British people, and especially Londoners, felt that they were at the centre of a huge empire. Our wealth and political power had increased for over 200 years, partly because of our manufacturing industry, our important role in world trade and the development of our coal industry.

Things are very different for us in the 21st century. We have lost our empire and have reverted to being merely a group of small islands on the edge of Europe.

Our manufacturing industry has declined. Although we have experienced tremendous technological changes since the war, we are faced with the fundamental problem of how to provide ourselves with energy.

We still cannot decide how to find a balance between using coal, oil, and nuclear-energy, and also renewable energy such as wind-power, hydro-electric power and solar energy.

In 1948 my mother continued the routine which she had followed before and during the war. We sat down to Sunday dinner at 1.00 pm, while listening to the radio, and ate the left-over meat on Monday evening.

On Monday morning my mother did the week's washing: clothes or bed-linen were boiled in the large copper vat which stood in the kitchen. After squeezing most of the water out of them by putting them through a mangle, my mother put them on a wooden 'horse' to dry in front of our coal or electric fire in the living room. We didn't have central heating, and I doubt if we needed to use as much electricity as is needed in modern households.

During the war the Government had produced several slogans, which included: "*Careless talk costs lives,*" "*Is your journey really necessary?*" and "*Make do and mend.*" Our wartime culture had been one of a grim determination to survive, and this included the idea of being careful and wasting as little as possible. This spirit continued for some time after the war had ended.

My mother's photo, taken in our living room at some time during the war, reflects this culture (overleaf). You can see bare floor-boards under a thread-bare carpet. She is knitting some sort of garment – probably a pair of socks or a woollen pullover. She spent a lot of her spare time knitting and this remained an important activity for her for the rest of her life, because it saved money.

The oak sideboard contained our best crockery and glassware. On top of it you can see a biscuit barrel and the box containing our best cutlery. (This last had been a wedding present and I still have it in our kitchen in North London.) Just in front of it is the wooden box in which mother kept the tobacco which she retrieved from her cigarette-ends, so that she could make more cigarettes.

Most significant of all is the expression on mother's face. She doesn't look at all happy. Why is this?

Her appearance indicates that she was under considerable strain during the war. Generally speaking, those British people who are under the age of 65 have no idea what it is like to suffer from bombing raids.

So far we have been lucky since World War Two: our armed forces have bombed other parts of the world, but no other country has bombed us. Need I say more?

20 Our Living Room
During the war, and in the first few years afterwards, our possessions and our way of life remained simple. We had a radio and a gramophone, but no television until I went into the army in 1955.

15 Religion and Church Services

In 1900 England was indubitably a Christian country but our society has changed considerably in this respect since the Second World War. Partly because of the influence of modern scientific ideas many more English people than before are atheists or agnostics.

After 1949 a great many West Indian immigrants came to live and work in the British Isles, and many of them were committed Christians, thus strengthening our traditional religion. However, many other immigrants were Hindus and Muslims, and their two ways of life are very different from traditional Christianity. Buddhist, Taoist and Zen ideologies have also taken root here, and Judaism has, of course, been a way of life for some people here for centuries.

We can say that the Christian Church in England was already fragmented in 1900; Roman Catholicism, the Church of England, and various sects of Protestant Christianity were well established. Nevertheless, it seems to me that in the 21st century our society is even more fragmented culturally than before.

This is not necessarily a bad thing. One philosophical idea is that *"Thesis and (its opposite) Antithesis lead to Synthesis,"* and that this can help in the development of worthwhile ideas. If this is correct then our rich cultural mix should be beneficial. However, whereas some parts of our English society are tolerant, there are too many people who cannot bear the idea of living alongside other groups who are very different.

This wasn't such a problem in 1948! It was assumed that most people belonged to the Church of England. Church and State were still connected insofar that many schools and other social groups had close relationships with particular churches. I can remember attending special services both at *All Saints Church* and at *St. James's Church* (photos overleaf).

I took part in special services at *All Saints Church* because I was a Cub. Every so often there would be a Church Parade in which Scouts, Girl-Guides, Cubs and Brownies would enter the church in a procession, together with the flags and banners which indicated their particular troops. I also attended the occasional special service at *St. James's Church* because I was a pupil at *St. James's School*.

Now there is far less connection between Church and State than there used to be. In 2013 it was decided to change the oath taken by boy-scouts and girl-guides so that they don't have to express a belief in God. This change would have been unthinkable before the Second World War.

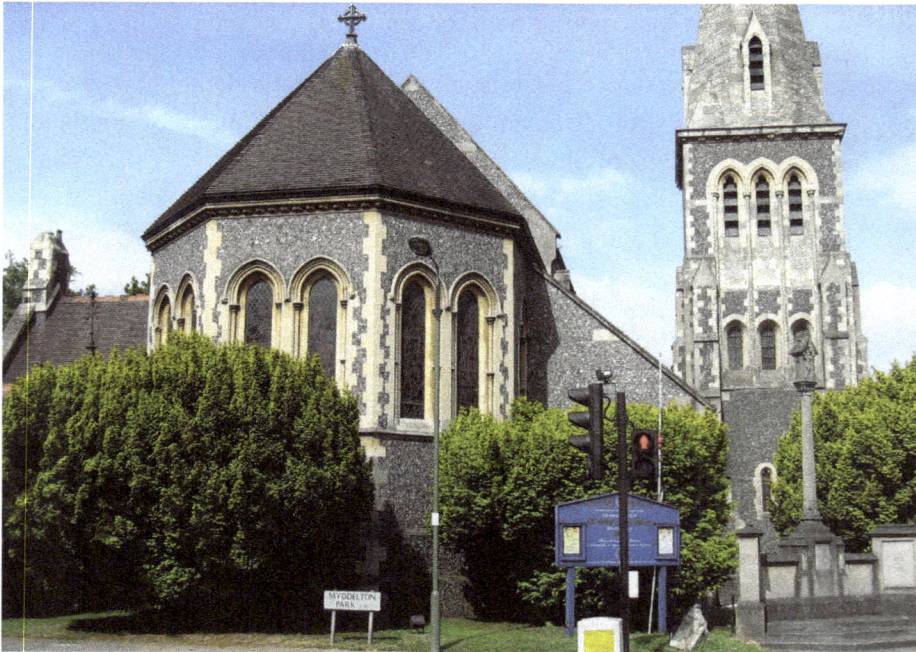

21 All Saints Church
This is a modern photo from 2009 which shows the church which I attended until I ceased to be a Christian.

22 St. James's Church
This is situated next to Friern Barnet Lane, which used to be the thoroughfare from London to the North before the new highway was created by way of Finchley Common.

16 Culture and Conflict

The British Isles have been home to a variety of cultures since before historical times, but until recently they were mostly brought by immigrants from the European area. Since World War II, however, a great many immigrants have come from all over the world. This has enriched our country in a variety of ways, but has also increased the possibility of conflict within our society. Is such conflict natural? The answer is "Yes!" Is such conflict desirable? The answer must surely be "No!"

Several centuries ago, a Chinese statesman stated: *"Our humanity brings us together, but our cultures drive us apart."*

Each human being is unique and this can be shown by employing a branch of modern mathematics. Boolean algebra has provided us with a new way to think about logical processes and Venn diagrams can be used to illustrate such ideas.

In the Venn diagram opposite it can be seen that group A consists of people who have played chess but don't like eating curry and don't speak Welsh. The people in group B have played chess and like curry, but don't speak Welsh, whereas those in group C have played chess as well as liking curry and speaking Welsh.

This kind of analysis indicates that, apart from identical twins, no two people can be exactly the same, since each one of us must be a member of thousands of different sets which overlap. It is possible that even identical twins will differ from each other in some ways.

Editor's Note The idea that identical twins may not be identical not only for environmental reasons is explored in a wonderful book written for the general reader entitled *The Hidden Half* by M.Blastland (2019). This book describes numerous studies that have shown around half of the variation between individuals in many species, including *Homo sapiens,* cannot be explained by *any* systematic factors, genetic or environmental—hence the intriguing title.

From this it can be seen that each human being has his or her own culture which is the product of genetic make-up and social conditioning. Our parents and siblings (or lack of them) provide us with our first cultural background and so the potential for conflict first exists within the family. As we grow older, we are influenced by our local community, our educational system (or lack of it), our working conditions and the nature of the country in which we live.

The likelihood of conflict exists at each level, and therefore we all need to learn to think clearly and to discuss problems sensibly. Most people around the world agree that they want what is good, but they don't all agree as to what constitutes *"The Good."* That is why I say *"When the talking stops, the stones start to fly."* It's a great pity that so many people are unable to *"Live – and let live."*

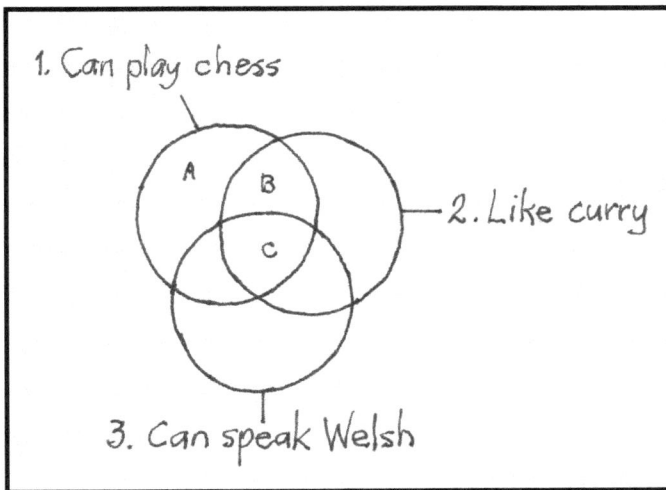

23 A Venn Diagram
This illustrates the idea in the text. It indicates how someone can be in a variety of overlapping groups. As there are countless groups in the world, it would be impossible for anyone to be in all of them, which proves that each person is unique.

17 Physical Training

When I was eleven I didn't have the faintest idea about the importance of cultural conditioning. I wasn't aware that I was a prisoner trapped in a particular body in a particular place at a particular time. I was too involved with enjoying my life at home and at school. Although I was an avid reader and spent a lot of time learning about the world around me, I was also physically active.

It seems that in the 1930s the government had become worried that our population wasn't as fit as some of the people on the continent, such as those in Germany and Sweden. A National Fitness Campaign was started in 1937 and young children like me benefited as a result of it.

I've already mentioned that we were expected to play football and go swimming as part of our weekly curriculum, but for these activities we had to leave the school premises. Our teachers also took us into the school playground so that we could play games and undertake physical exercises. PT (physical training) was the phrase used when I was younger, both at primary school and at my grammar school, but later PE (physical exercise) became the more acceptable expression.

Physical training was an apt description because it included various movements which were designed to use and strengthen a variety of muscles in our body. We spread out and then followed the teacher's instructions as to which exercises to perform. One such exercise was to jump so that our feet were apart and then back with them together while at the same time raising and lowering our arms. This form of exercise is sometimes called doing *star jumps*.

After warming up with what were sometimes called *Swedish Exercises* we would then play some energetic games. I certainly benefited from a great deal of exercise when I was young.

18 Old Books

I enjoyed physical exercise and took it for granted that, wherever possible, I would walk rather than use public transport, but I was also a bookworm!

In 1948 printed books, with hardback linen covers, were part of our culture and had been so since the 15th century. William Caxton introduced the technique of printing books into England in 1476. Now in the 21st century they are being superseded by 'electronic books.' It is possible to download hundreds of texts into a machine which is about the same size as a pocket-sized book. This is yet another technological revolution which will be of immense help in some ways, but it means that we may no longer produce traditional books, which can be beautiful artefacts. It would be a pity if traditional hardback books were allowed to die out. In fact, there is little sign of this at present. People like books.

I have four hardback books which were given to my mother at the beginning of the 20th century and each one is a work of art in its own right. Apart from enjoying the stories I also found pleasure in looking at the pictures, which probably added to my artistic education. I must also mention the book which I believe to have been the first which I bought for myself. It has been on my shelf for most of my life, and although it's a paperback I still consider it to be beautiful: it involves Professor Branestawm.

(1) *The Zoo Past and Present* was published in London in 1905. There were no photographs but the book contained 103 illustrations by A.T. Elwes, who wrote the text with some help from the Reverand Theodore Wood. The pictures had been printed from engravings and each engraving had been produced from a drawing which included a great deal of cross-hatching as a way of providing shading. I have used this technique in some of my own drawings.

The 147 pages contained twenty-one chapters with titles such as The Lion House, The Monkey House and The Bears' Cages. Each chapter provided both biological and historical information but also included a number of anecdotes. For example, one anecdote in Chapter One described how a brave zoo-keeper, Mr. Cocksedge, saved two tiger cubs from being eaten by their mother. Another anecdote told of how a chimpanzee called Sally was able to count up to five, six or seven in order to obtain a reward.

24 Sally
It was said that this chimpanzee showed signs of being able to count up to eight.

A gruesome story concerned an eleven-foot python which was discovered to have swallowed its companion; the latter had been only two feet shorter!

Chapter Six, *The Elephant House,* included the history of Jumbo, the famous elephant who arrived at the zoo in about 1878. He became one of the public's favourite animals but was sometimes very dangerous and so was eventually sold to Barnum, the American showman. Sadly, soon after arriving in the United States, Jumbo was killed by a train while crossing a railway line.

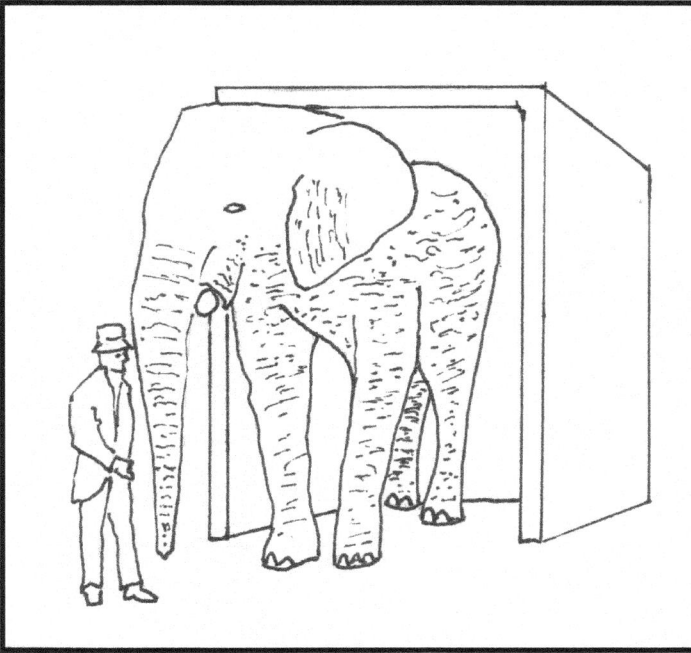

25 Jumbo and His Keeper Jumbo was the largest elephant in London Zoo at that time and so he needed a very large packing-case when he was transported to the United States of America.

(2) ***The Witch's Kitchen*** appears to have been published in 1910. It was written by Gerald Young, but what made it a beautiful book in my eyes were the illustrations by Willy Pogany. He was a Hungarian artist who came to London from Budapest in about 1905. There were nine chapters in the book's 226 pages, but there were also 79 illustrations; i.e. there was roughly a picture on one page in three. Pogany seems to have been influenced by *Art Nouveau.* He was able to imbue each scene

with a sense of movement and often introduced giant dandelion patterns as semi-abstract designs. I hope that some of my own pen-and-ink sketches will have a similar lively quality.

26 The Witch and the Children
In *The Witch's Kitchen* she entices the two little girls away from their bedroom by letting them ride on beautiful broomsticks.

The story involved two little girls, Dulcie and Doris, who were stolen from their beds by a witch. They were rescued by two boys, Frank and Rollo, the latter for a while having been turned into a toad. They were also helped by Mr. Springy, an indiarubber man!

(3) *Over the Nonsense Road* was also published in 1910. This copy was given to my mother for her ninth birthday in 1917. It had 234 pages and seven watercolour illustrations by F. Strothmann. It was

divided into five stories, each of which featured an animal: The *Jolly Bruang* (Bruin was a popular name for a bear in children's stories), The *Gay Baboon* (gay meant bright, carefree and merry at that time) and *Grandmother Marmot* (a prairie dog) were the central figures in the first three stories. The *Courtly Peeshoo* and the *Witching Wah* in the final two stories might have been a lynx and a raccoon respectively.

27 A Mermaid on a Dolphin
This beautiful picture is a good example of the artwork in *Over the Nonsense Road.*

Each story consisted of from four to six chapters, and the author, Lucile Gulliver, wrote them in a very flowing and poetical style. There was a great deal of repetition of individual words and phrases. Each story was rather like an extended folk story or fairy tale. In this respect they remind me of *"The King of the Golden River"* by John Ruskin, but *"Over the Nonsense Road"* has so many passages which are inconsequential that they are almost surreal.

It would have appealed to young children because it included a large number of animals such as cats and mice, a mole, a beaver, cows, puppies and various birds. It also included everyday activities such as cooking, washing, sewing and other housework. It was probably meant to be read to children, but I was able to read it for myself.

(4) *The Girl's Holiday Book* was reprinted in 1917 and my mother received it as a prize in 1922 when she was thirteen years old. This was because she had been a regular attender at Young Peoples Services, Victoria Hall, Wandsworth. The book had been edited by Mrs. Herbert Strang and displayed a strong Christian ethos. It contained twelve stories, two poems and a set of quotations, but the pages were not numbered and there was no table of contents!

Several of the stories were set in foreign countries: the heroine in the first story, *"Paulina's Adventure,"* was a Russian girl who helped the Emperor when he was lost in a forest; while the second story was about a mean Baghdad merchant who suffered disasters when he tried to throw away his old slippers.

Some of the stories featured girls who showed courage and determination or who wanted to help other people. The information and ideas presented to me were interesting but I also enjoyed the illustrations which were in a variety of styles.

(5) *The Incredible Adventures of Professor Branestawm* was written by Norman Hunter and first published in 1933, but I first discovered it while I was visiting Uncle Tom, Auntie Margaret and Cousin Pamela at their flat on Canvey Island, Essex, in July 1948. I noticed it in a nearby bookshop and what attracted me to it was the artwork. The artist, W. Heath Robinson, was skilful at creating absurd pictures which matched the nonsense stories about the absent-minded professor.

One chapter, entitled *The Wild Waste Paper*, recounted what happened when the professor's housekeeper accidentally caused a bottle of liquid to bring to life the papers in a waste-paper basket.

Another story, *The Professor Borrows a Book*, described how he lost several copies of a public library book, *The Life and Likings of a Lobster*, because he classified them in different ways on his bookshelves. He put one copy under 'Biographies,' another under 'Deep Sea Diving' and so on. As I grew older, I came to realise that this was not as incredible as it seemed. The more information we acquire the more difficult it becomes to store it in such a way that we can retrieve it easily. Here was another book which stimulated my imagination and gave me artistic pleasure.

Abou Cassem and the magistrate

28 Abou Cassem
He was a Baghdad merchant who experienced a series of misadventures while trying to rid himself of his old slippers. Here we see him complaining to the Cadi of his troubles.

19 ... and Why Read?

Why have I written so much about books? The answer is very simple. It takes a long time to have adventures. Men and women who go adventuring spend a lot of time eating, sleeping, washing and engaging in a variety of other everyday activities. The exciting events which happen to them take place only from time to time. A capable storyteller concentrates on the interesting and exciting parts of an adventure story, links these episodes together skilfully and omits most of the mundane details.

For example, it took Marco Polo twenty years for him to travel from Italy to China and back again. He left Venice with his father and uncle in the 13th century, and after his return he was captured in a battle and eventually dictated the story of his experiences to a fellow prisoner while in prison. It took me only a week or so to read his story while I was still young. I therefore had the benefit of learning from his experiences without the bother of travelling for many years and without the need to endure all that he had to suffer.

What is true of fiction is also true of non-fiction: a skilful writer can impart information which might take the learner weeks, months or even years to acquire. Not only that! A well-written manual may prove to be just as good as some teachers – and could well be much cheaper.

A tremendous amount of my knowledge and understanding has come about because of my love of reading. This in turn has helped me to understand and enjoy the things which have happened to me. Reading has also helped me to make decisions as to what I should do with my time when I'm not reading. We need to be able to read well in order to educate ourselves - the only true education. You may complain that we cannot be certain as to whether or not the items which we read are true. This is a valid point to make – but who says that life has to be easy?

29 Marco Polo
This picture comes from the 13th century and shows
Marco Polo with a companion while on his travels in
foreign countries.

20 My Artistic Ability

I enjoyed drawing from an early age but I didn't have much imagination for drawing and painting when I was young. I found it easier to copy some of the pictures in newspapers and to paint over the printed pictures in some books.

For example, I copied pictures of motor cars in the *Buck Ryan* comic strip in the Daily Mirror; and I enjoyed painting over a Mountie (a Royal Canadian Mounted Policeman) in one of my *Chatterbox* annuals, so much so that I later painted over it again and spoiled it! However, I did develop the ability to copy pictures accurately and so I suppose that my hand-eye co-ordination became better.

On Wednesday 17th March 1948 my elocution teacher, Miss Stanley, lent me a book about Greek gods and I copied some pictures from it. They were only outline drawings – there was no shading involved – and when I showed them to a class-mate he said that I must have traced them. I protested that I was innocent of any such action but he still didn't believe me.

I also improved my ability to use coloured pencils and I remember that I was very disappointed in a young teacher who took us for a History lesson during my final year or so. She must have been a student or perhaps a supply teacher. She showed us her picture of a Norman knight which she had copied from our text-book; she had coloured it in and held it up to show us, and it looked good from a distance. When I took my picture to show her what I had done, I noticed that her coloured shading wasn't as good as mine.

When I thought about this many years later, I realised that she had done it without spending much time over it in order to show us what she wanted us to do, but at the time it made me feel more confident in my own artistic ability!

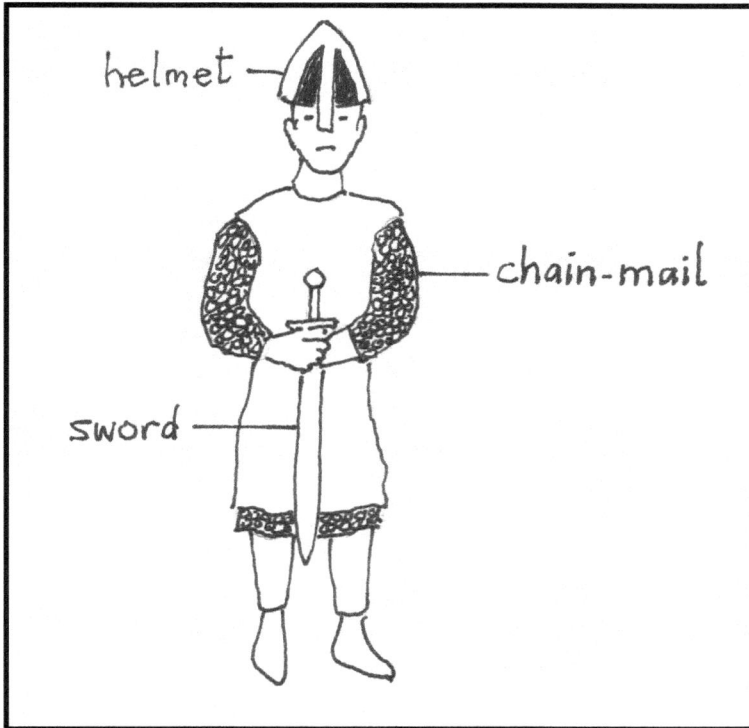

30 A Norman Knight
This is the kind of picture which we were shown at Primary
School. It helped to give us the idea that the Past is not
the same as the Present.

21 A School Journey

My artistic ability also benefited when I went on a school trip to St. Mary's Bay Holiday Camp which lasted from Friday 11th until Friday25th June 1948. The camp was on the south coast and we made our way there by coach. My mother had to take my ration book to Miss Leroy two days before we left since basic foodstuffs were still rationed.

Our group of boys slept in a brick hut with a partition down the middle of it and there were pupils from another school on the other side. We were expected to make notes and draw pictures during some of our activities and we then copied them neatly into a special booklet which was our diary. Unfortunately, I threw this booklet away many years ago, but I can remember drawing a seagull, and some shells from the beach, amongst other things.

We visited Canterbury Cathedral and the *Dungeness Lighthouse*, as well as travelling on the *Romney, Hythe and Dymchurch Light Railway*. I still have the postcard which I gave to my father showing the *"World's Smallest Railway at St. Mary's Bay, Kent."* We also visited Dover Castle and screamed when we thought that we were going to be locked in the dungeons!

This was the first and only time that I went away from home on a school journey, and I regret to say that I was not always well-behaved.

My friend, John Browne, invented a game called *"Under the Lashing Blanket."* This involved several boys cramming themselves onto a bed and covering themselves with a single blanket between them while John or someone else hit them with a leather belt.

To be fair to John, he did enjoy being one of those on the bed. It created a lot of movement and generated a great deal of noise as we struggled to evade the whip. It's not surprising that a teacher came in

31 The Romney, Hythe and Dymchurch Light Railway
I remember that I enjoyed travelling on this narrow-gauge
railway, because its carriages were smaller than usual,
and so it had a cosy feel to it.

to complain on more than one occasion, but it is surprising that the bed
didn't collapse under the weight of four or five small boys! (John's
photo is in *Memory 2*; see also the *Postscript,* p.189.)

22 *Where was I in 1948?*

I didn't realise it at the time, but at the age of eleven I was already a very lucky boy. I hadn't been born dead on arrival. I was born without any great physical defects—apart from being short-sighted—and although I needed glasses from an early age, I could have survived without their aid. My mother didn't die in childbirth and my parents managed to live together for well over thirty years without feeling the need to get divorced. (Apparently my father struck my mother once in the early days of their marriage, and she told him that if he did that again she would leave him.) He did strike me with a belt, but that occurred only on two, or at the most, three occasions.

Despite the Second World War I starved only once as a young boy, and that was when I wasn't allowed to eat for several days because of some illness or other. Neither my parents nor I were killed or injured during the war, nor were we bombed out of our flat.

My mother helped me to learn to read and I was physically, emotionally and intellectually intelligent enough to cope with the strain of going to school, mixing with other people, and responding to all the demands of school life.

I was a human being living in a democratic country on the outskirts of one of the greatest capital cities on Planet Earth in the mid-20th century. Some biologists will tell you that much of my good fortune lay in my genes, but it must also be true that my family, school and national cultures gave me a good start in life. I was a prisoner trapped in a particular body in space and time, but the time and place of my birth meant that I had a chance to come to terms with my limitations and to develop my personality.

Every day I am aware of how lucky I have been!

32 The Author at the End of his Primary Education
I had enjoyed my time at St. James's Church of England
School but was now looking ahead with pleasure to my
Secondary Education.

23 My Parents and I

In 1948 I was extremely fortunate because my parents and I had survived the Second World War without undue suffering – at least as far as I was concerned. I had received a good basic education both at home and at three schools. My parents were strict in what they demanded of me: they expected me to work hard and behave myself, and to consider the wishes of others.

As taught by Jesus Christ, Confucius, Buddha and other thinkers they wanted me to behave towards other people in the same way that I would want others to behave towards me. But they never told me what to think.

The Germans say, "*Die Gedanken sind frei,*" which means, "*Thoughts are free, or we can think freely,*" but this is only true if we are not subjected to propaganda.

Thanks to a variety of fiction and non-fiction books, together with my beloved encyclopaedias, I was able to investigate the world around me. I was still under the influence of my parents and society in general but I was also able to think for myself to some extent. Of course, it was only after several years at grammar school that I really began to think for myself.

I remember two incidents which occurred towards the end of my time at Junior School.

We were discussing films in class and Arthur Jewell mentioned that he had seen an adventure film which showed the kinds of shoes and clothing worn by the Mongols who invaded China. I felt sceptical about the film-makers' accuracy and thought that he was being too trusting.

On another occasion a teacher read a story to us in which someone died in his or her sleep because of a dream. We were expected to think that it was impossible for this story to be true, but I didn't think of this aspect because, from my experience of books, I assumed that a storyteller was able to be god-like.

These two events seem to indicate that at the age of eleven I was both cynical and idealistic.

24 Another Turning Point

As I've grown older, I've come to understand the importance of 'chance' (i.e. random factors) in our lives. In theory we start off with the opportunity of developing in any direction: *"Anyone can do anything."* In fact, this isn't true at all. The time, manner and place of our birth determine to a large extent what opportunities lie before us. Our future doesn't lie in the stars. It lies within ourselves, but also depends on many factors which are beyond our control.

The development of our life is like the structure of a tree. As we grow older, we begin to follow a path which is similar to the way that a branch grows out from a tree trunk and then develops smaller and smaller branches and then twigs. Sometimes we can move from one branch to another, but such sideways movements are not easy and are therefore unusual. If we change direction suddenly it is usually because of chance events which come from outside ourselves.

Of course, I had no knowledge of this in 1948 at the age of eleven. It wasn't until I reached college in 1957 that I first began to think seriously about 'free will.' Looking back, however, I can see that 1948 was another turning point in my life in so far that I was given the opportunity to attend a good, local grammar school. This made a great difference to my future prospects.

I was too busy following my interests to be aware of this. At that time, I hadn't heard of the old Latin saying *"Carpe diem,"* which tells people to enjoy, and make the most of, each day as if it were a flower waiting to be plucked.

I was fortunate indeed that I was able to enjoy my life from day to day in relative peace and security, and in the summer of 1948, I was able to look forward to the future with confidence and hope. I knew that I was entering a new and important stage of my life.

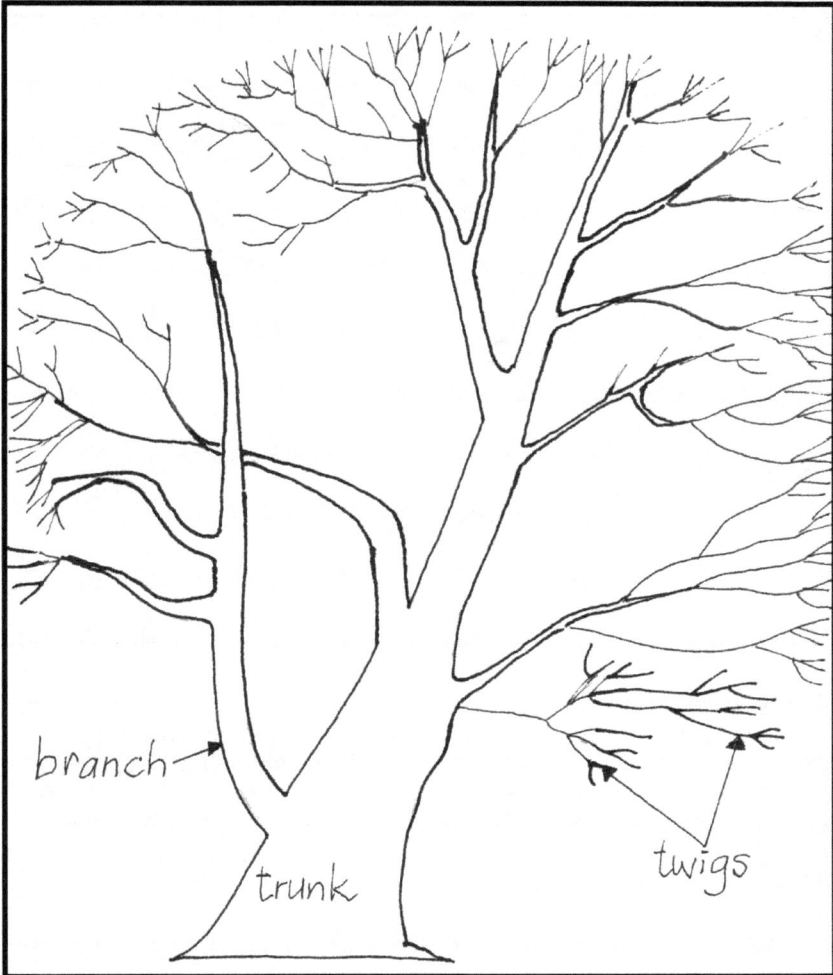

33 An Oak Tree

This is an abstract diagram, both of an oak tree and of the way that our life can change as though we were travelling along the trunk, branches and twigs of a tree. Unlike a squirrel which can jump easily from branch to branch, it is not easy for us to change direction once we have begun to move along one branch, and it seems that most people don't make fundamental changes of direction more than a few times.

34 My Janus Pot

Janus was the Roman god of doorways, passages and bridges. He was usually depicted as having two heads which looked in opposite directions. Our word January comes from his name, and the Old Year and the New Year are often represented as an old man and a baby. I made this pot many years ago to show the two faces of an old man and a baby.

I have now reached the end of Book 2 of *Curious Bear* (apart from the Postscript that follows next). Book 2 has reviewed the events up to 1948 and my life thereafter will have to await a Book 3. The *Janus* pot illustration above is a way of signalling this turning point. The beginning of a new era in my life lies ahead.

Postscript

A Short History of
John Stanley Browne

John Stanley Browne

John was born about three weeks after me, on 7th December 1936, and was evacuated to Leeds during the Second World War. Although he went with his mother, two sisters and a brother, he didn't enjoy his time there.

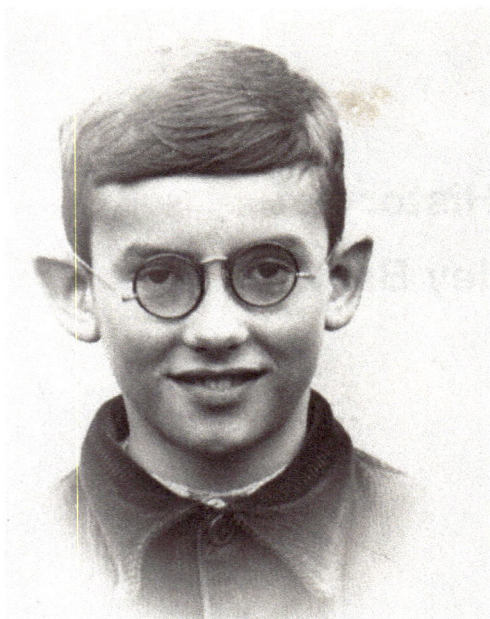

1 John in 1948

When he returned to London, he went to live at 6, Miles Way, which was about half a mile uphill from my parents' flat. He joined St. James's Primary School which is where he met me and my other best friend, Frederick Murphy. The three of us became close friends and later went to Woodhouse Grammar School where we were put into the same class. His mother was a widow and so John left Woodhouse in 1953, at the end of the Fifth Form, so that he could help to support his family financially.

While we were at Woodhouse School, he and I visited each other's homes several times. My father had several jazz records from the 1930s and I believe that it was due to his influence that John began to be interested in this style of music. Although he also enjoyed classical music it was jazz which really enthused him for the rest of his life.

In **2,** John is on the left standing on a bridge with Tony Regan. They were on our school trip to Cambridge at the end of the Fifth Form.

John's first work may have been in banking or insurance, but he then went into the Army and became a bomb disposal specialist. After finishing his National Service, he eventually went to work for Randall's of Potters Bar – a firm which specialised in selling toys and other items of interest to children. However, he didn't lose touch with his old school friends.

2 John in 1953

Photo **3,** I believe, was taken a few years after John had left Woodhouse School.

3 John in 1950s

While I was in the Upper Sixth Form, I began to visit Wood Green Jazz Club with John and two other classmates – Brian Smith and Tony Regan. I also introduced them to Arthur Fossey who was in the year below me at Woodhouse. I got to know him because we were in a combined History group once per week. He and I used to walk home from school in the hot summer of 1955, heatedly discussing jazz until we reached his prefab* close to Bethune Park. He joined our group of jazz fans and so we had the nucleus of a group who remained friends and later met frequently for a number of years.

4 John with Three Friends

I don't know who his female friend was in **4**, nor why they each had a parrot.

While I was undertaking my National Service in faraway Cyprus, 1955-1957, John continued to meet Brian and Arthur. The latter introduced John to Jim Harrington, who was a fellow member of the St. John's Ambulance Brigade. Arthur also introduced Mike Watson, who was a quantity surveyor. Somehow or other they became friendly with Laurie Sparey, who was also a Woodhouse pupil, and whose father owned a small cabin craft, *Alor Star* **4**, on the River Lea.

Brian and Arthur sent me photographs which made me very envious of their lives because they indicated that they were enjoying life by playing about on the boat on the River Lea and attending numerous jazz concerts in town, while I was stuck at the far end of the Mediterranean.

5 The *Alor Star*

From left to right: Brian Smith, Laurie Sparey, Joan Greenfield and the author. John is hanging on the back.

When I returned from Cyprus, I re-joined the group and met them frequently when I was at home from college. I began to join them several times a week in order to go to a variety of local public-houses, where we drank beer and played darts or dominoes. We also visited jazz concerts and began to attend Barnet Jazz Club which hosted traditional bands such as Ken Colyer and Acker Bilk.

During my vacations from college I joined John and the others who had bought the hull of a small boat which they kept at a boatyard on the River Lea. For several years we gradually built it into a simple cabin craft with an outboard motor. This was thanks to Laurie Sparey who was studying as a designer and jeweller. He was the leader of the group in this project because of his design skills.

6 Working on the boat
From left to right: Mike Watson, Joan Greenfield and Laurie
Sparey. John is in the distance on the right. We started our
project by covering the hull with fibre-glass, but much of our time
was spent in the local pub!

John was always at the social centre of our group because of his
intelligence and his lively personality. Laurie's girl-friend, Joan
Greenfield, was the other centre of our group. We developed a routine
of meeting up at her parents' house on a Friday evening before going to
a pub. Often we would return to the house to chat until the early hours
of the morning. When she and Laurie married, she continued to be a
charming hostess, and for some years *The Boys* continued to meet at her
home after visiting such pubs as *The Builders* in East Barnet.

7 John, the Salesman
John's body and body-language indicates that he enjoyed eating and drinking. He was a *bon viveur*!

Soon after joining Randall's John was sent abroad as a salesman for the firm. He flew to Africa, the Middle East and as far afield as Singapore and Australia. These trips took place in the spring, usually from mid-January until March, and for the first few years we celebrated his departure and his return. He sent a great many hastily written letters to Joan, who then let us all read them. He was clearly a very successful salesman, and he was always an amusing conversationalist with a ready wit. He enjoyed repartee.

I continued to see him quite often for some years after I married Pat Mould. The two of us continued to go out with *The Boys* for some time but I drifted apart from the group once Pat and I had become parents. John never married. This was, perhaps, because he wanted to be able to follow his own inclinations.

John continued his work with Randall's for the rest of his career, but after his mother died, he moved to a flat in Friern Barnet Lane. Apart from his love of jazz, he also became a supporter of the Edinburgh Festival and for many years he would travel north to enjoy the variety of performances on offer.

I met him just a few weeks before he died. We were walking towards each other not far from the top of Friern Barnet Lane and each of us was holding something in our right hands. We fumbled to shake hands and then used our left hands clumsily. I immediately said, *"People will think that we're Masons!"* This was typical of the jokes which had bound us together for over sixty years.

"Thank you, John, it was a pleasure to know you!"

8 John in 2009

Notes

The following *Notes* are referred

to with asterisks * in the text. They

are intended to help the reader with

unusual or difficult words or phrases,

by giving some background or

historical information about them.

Chapter 1

Memory 1, page 4 ...the Middle Ages...

Broadly speaking, this term refers to the period between the end of the Roman Empire and the start of the Italian Renaissance, i.e. about 450-1450 AD. More narrowly, in England, it refers to the period between the Norman Conquest (1066) and the 15th Century.

Memory 1, page 4 ...Chipping Barnet...

Chipping comes from Old English and refers to buying and selling goods. Merchants held a market at High Barnet, so called because of its situation at the top of a steep hill. It is not the same as the modern Borough of Barnet which covers a much larger area of North London.

Memory 3, page 9 ...Secondary Modern School.

Secondary education followed on from Primary education and was for pupils aged from eleven. A Secondary Modern School provided pupils with practical, vocational work and was less academic than a grammar school.

Memory 4, page 10 May I say...

The Headmaster didn't put a question mark at the end of his first sentence. This was because it was not really a question. It was a polite command, or even a simple statement! I do the same thing, but usually add the word 'please,' e.g. "Could you please send it to me tomorrow."

Memory 4, page 11 ...Cockney...

This comes from Old English and means a cockerel's egg. It has come to mean a working-class person from the East End of London, and also their culture and language. It's possible that the Cockney accent has descended from one dialect of Anglo-Saxon.

Memory 5, page 12 Firstly, ...

Nowadays only a few authors use the adverbs 'firstly, secondly' etc., when introducing ideas in a sequence of sentences. I do this because these ordinal numbers are being used to qualify sentences and therefore should be adverbs. Most writers nowadays use the adjectives 'first, second, third,' but this sounds wrong to my ears. Fowler (1926) seems to agree with me. Fowler (2004) suggests that the best solution to the problem is to use 'First, secondly, thirdly…' i.e. a compromise!

Memory 8, page 18 …as long as…

Some writers also use "…so long as…"

Memory 10, page 23 Nowadays they would be pilloried…

A pillory (plural: pillories) was a wooden frame which was used in the Middle Ages to provide a punishment for offenders. Today, the phrase 'to be pilloried' refers to people being harshly criticised by the press and other media.

Memory 12, page 26 …Arabic or Roman numerals…

Our modern numbers (1, 2, 3, etc.) were brought to Europe from the East by Arabic traders. Until then Europeans had used numerals (I, II, III, IV, V etc.) from the Roman Empire, and they are still used occasionally today.

Memory 12, page 27 …dominoes was a very popular game…

Generally speaking, the verb in a simple sentence should match what follows it in the Predicate. That is why I have not written "Dominoes were a … game."

Memory 14, page 30 …Jack and the Beanstalk.

This is a well-know folk-tale in England. It concerns a small boy who buys some magic beans which his mother throws out of the window! Overnight they grow into a huge beanstalk which grows up as far as the clouds. Jack climbs the beanstalk and has several adventures which end when a giant chases him. Jack climbs down the beanstalk, seizes an axe, and chops the stalk so that it topples down and kills the giant. This story has become a popular subject for English pantomimes.

Memory 14, page 30 ...Snow White and the Seven Dwarves...

This story comes from the series of folk-tales collected by two German brothers: Jakob Ludwig Grimm (1785-1863) and Wilhelm Karl Grimm (1786-1859). This is another popular subject for English pantomime.

Memory 14, page 31 ...had been laid down...

Many English people remain confused by the verbs 'to lie (down)' and 'to lay.' I lie on the floor (present); I lay on the floor (past); I have lain on the floor (perfect tense). I lay down my pen (present); I laid down my pen (past); I have laid down my pen (perfect tense).

Memory 14, page 31 ...crossword puzzle...

This type of puzzle consists of numbered clues for words which are to be fitted into a grid of rows and columns of boxes. A letter of the alphabet is written into each box. As the reader fills in the missing words, some of them are found to cross each other, and this helps the reader to solve the clues.

Memory 18, page 38 ...Rudyard Kipling (1865-1936)

He was English but was born in India and became a poet, writer of short stories and a novelist. He was given the Nobel Prize for literature in 1907. His two Jungle Books (1894 and 1895) included animal characters, some of which became titles of leadership within the Boy Scout movement. Stalky and Co (1899) described the adventures of a group of boys at boarding school in England. The Just So Stories (1902) were modern fairy stories, such as "How the elephant got his nose."

Memory 18, page 38 The Jungle Book...

Its hero was Mowgli, 'the little frog,' who was brought up by a wolf-pack in India. His friends included a panther and a bear, but his chief enemy was a tiger.

Memory 18, page 38 Firstly...

See the explanation for Memory 5, page 12.

Memory 18, page 38 British Bulldog...

The bulldog is a muscular and aggressive dog which is thought to be good at holding on to animals bigger than itself. Long ago it became a symbol of British power and tenacity – especially in political cartoons. Punch, the 19th and 20th century satirical magazine, included a bulldog on its title page.

Memory 18, page 38 ...the traditional British thin red line."

For over a hundred years it was the custom for British soldiers to wear red uniforms. It seems that this was to hide the sight of blood. British soldiers were therefore called 'Redcoats.' If they marched forward to attack an enemy, they presented a red line across the landscape. In the film "The Four Feathers," an ex-general describes the Charge of the Light Brigade during the Crimean War, draws a line of wine across the table and says, "Here is the thin red line."

Chapter 2

Memory 1, page 48 "...'Thank you for having me' when you leave the party."

I don't like the modern method of using inverted commas to indicate speech. Fowler (1926) states: there is no universally accepted distinction between the single form ('...') and the double ("...") but he goes on to say: the more sensible practice is to regard the single as normal. Fowler

(2004) states: single marks are to be used for a first quotation; then double for a quotation within a quotation. I disagree. Reading is a difficult skill and needs to be made as easy as possible. My experience and the books on my shelves indicate that double quotation marks were used as the primary way of showing speech for books published up until World War II. This made it easy to see that speech was being quoted. The modern way in England is unhelpful.

Memory 1, page 50 ...Oliver Twist.

He is one of Dickens' most famous characters. The novel of that name tells of how he was brought up in a workhouse. He was sent as a boy to work for an undertaker, where he was bullied by a bigger boy. Eventually he grew angry and thrashed the bully.

Memory 2, page 51 Japanese Karate Chinese Kong Fu.

Up until the end of the 19th century it was the English custom for boys and men to fight with their fists. The magazine Punch once had a cartoon which showed a ship's officer holding out boxing gloves towards two non-English sailors who were fighting with knives! Gunji Koizumi brought Judo to England in about 1905 when the Budokwai opened in London. Other martial arts gradually became better known in the British Isles during the 20th century. Karate, French Savate, and Thai boxing include kicking as part of their techniques. Kung Fu and Tai Chi also became better known to British people after World War II.

Memory 3, page 52 ...Wimbledon..

The famous Tennis championships, singles and doubles, are held annually at the Wimbledon Lawn Tennis Club.

Memory 3, page 52 ... the North Circular Road.

This was a ring road to the north of London, which was built to provide a means of travelling quickly across London by avoiding the centre. Nevertheless, at times, the heavy traffic can make the journey along it extremely slow!

Memory 4, page 54 ... steam test...
This was presumably a test to check that there were no faults in the system, and that the steam-power was adequate to enable the locomotive to pull a heavy load.

Memory 4, page 54 ... my National Service in 1957.
After World War II, the government decided to 'call up' young men at the age of 18, so that they could be available for training by the armed forces. This was called National Service. When I reached the age of eighteen, I was required to become a member of either the Army, or the Navy or the Royal Air Force. I chose the Army. At that time, national service lasted for two years.

Memory 5, page 56 ...Southend Arterial Road.
This was the A12 (trunk road) which then became the A127 (T). It stretched from the eastern side of London to Southend-on-Sea. In some places the road surface was just plain concrete, unlike most English roads which were covered with asphalt. My father and I joined it in the Walthamstow area.

Memory 5, page 56 ...a squire helping a knight to remove his armour!
During the Middle Ages armour developed to such an extent that, for a time, knights were covered from head to toe in metal. They needed someone to dress them before a battle and to undress them afterwards – if they survived! My father's rubber waders were very heavy and stretched to his thighs. He couldn't take them off very easily and it wasn't very easy for me either. I had to wriggle the boot section several times in order to get each legging to come off his leg.

Memory 6, page 58 ...Hillcrest
This name reflects the bungalow's location – near the top, or crest, of the hill.

Memory 6, page 58 ...Glycena...

I don't know the derivation of this name. As Dave's wife, my Auntie Margaret, was from Ireland, it may be that the name was derived from Irish Gaelic, Ireland's original language

Memory 6, page 58 ...Kendorern.

It seems obvious that Uncle Ernie's bungalow was named after his elder son, Kenneth, his wife, Doris, and himself.

Memory 7, page 60 ...Canvey Island...

This is about four miles long by three miles wide. It lies about five miles west of Southend-on-Sea, just about where the River Thames meets the English Channel, and it is only two or three miles south-west of Pitsea.

Memory 9, page 66 ...the East End of London...

This area has long been a working-class district of the capital city. The usual wind direction in Southern England is from west to east, and smelly workshops and industries developed downwind of wealthier districts. Wealthy families gravitated towards the West End of London.

Memory 10, page 69 ...National Service.

See the explanation for Memory 4, page 54.

Memory 14, page 76 ...shoe box...

When we bought footwear at a shoe-shop, we were often given the box in which the shoes had been sent to the shop. These boxes were very useful for storing small objects such as booklets, letters, photos and other documents.

Memory 15, page 78 ...I only played it a few times...

This is a common way of using the word 'only.' Grammatically it is better English to say: "I played it only a few times," because this makes it clear that 'only' is qualifying 'a few times.'

Memory 16, page 80 ...Merchant Navy.

The word 'tattoo' comes from Tahiti, which is an island in the south-west Pacific. It describes the process of drawing patterns or pictures on someone's skin by making little holes and filling them with ink. In 18th Century some British sailors copied the idea, but it was never considered suitable for the majority of the British population. By the 21st Century, however, many people in the British Isles had come to consider it to be a meaningful part of their lives.

Memory 19, page 87 ...Health and Safety...

Since the Second World War some governments have become more aware of the need to consider the welfare of their population. Some laws have been passed to improve people's health and their safety. For example, anti-smoking legislation was introduced in order to protect people from the effects of smoking tobacco, and the equipment in playgrounds was re-designed to protect the safety of children when playing.

Chapter 3

Memory 1, page 92 ...in decimal currency...

Our money system changed in 1971. The new system was much simpler than before, because each pound was now divided into 100 pence. The decimal system was based on the number ten (from the Latin word for ten: 'decem'), whereas the previous system was based on a variety of numbers. Until 1971, a pound was divided into 240 pence. 12 pence were equal to one shilling and 20 shillings were equal to one pound. There had also been farthings; four farthings were equal to one penny. Money sums included the signs £ = libra (pound), s = solidus (shilling) and d = denarius (penny). School-children needed to spend a long time mastering these systems; e.g. £7-8-8d + £5-15-10d = £13-4-6d. Thank goodness we copied the European decimal system of money when we did!

Memory 1, page 92 ...prefabs...

These were single-storey houses which were built from wooden sections which had been constructed in advance elsewhere (prefabricated) and then taken to a site where they could be assembled. They were put together far more quickly and cheaply than could be done with traditional brick or stone houses. They were helpful and popular in England immediately after the Second World War.

Memory 4, page 98 ...CV...

Curriculum vitae (Latin: the course of one's life). This was a list of a person's educational achievements, and possibly also his-her work experience, when applying for a job.

Memory 5, page 100 ...AID (Aeronautical Inspection Directorate)

This was concerned with overseeing the developments in the construction of aeroplanes and their equipment.

Memory 9, page 110 ...station equipment.

This would probably have been filing cabinets and furniture at the AID branch office in Leicester. Military personnel are said to be stationed somewhere in the British Isles or abroad; they are 'posted to a station.' The Civil Service uses the word 'station' in the same way. 'Railway-station' is a later use of the word 'station.'

Memory 14, page 120 ...latch-key child

The idea behind this term is that some children need to have a key in order to open the front door when they return home, because their parents are out at work. Such children are thought to be deprived in some way. This was not so in my case; I felt a sense of freedom when left on my own. How could I be bored if I had books to read?

Chapter 4

Memory 1, page 136   ...Easter...

This was originally a pagan festival to celebrate the end of winter and the birth of new life. It was absorbed into the Christian religion as a festival to celebrate the resurrection of Jesus Christ.

Memory 1, page 136 ...Shrove Tuesday...

Shrove Tuesday was originally the last day before Christians undertook a forty-day period of fasting to commemorate Christ's fasting in the desert. This period was called Lent and we enjoyed pancakes on Shrove Tuesday because they represented a luxurious meal before a period of abstinence.

Memory 4, page 142 Granddad was a sidesman...,

A sidesman was a member of a church congregation. One of his duties was to collect donations of money from the congregation while a hymn was being sung during a church service. Several sidesmen walked around slowly with a small bag. Each one held the bag out by its handle so that each worshipper could drop coins, or a banknote, into it. After they had collected the money, the bags were put together onto a metal plate and taken to the priest. [*Editor's Note:* According to Google NGram, in British English the spelling "grandad" is more popular than "granddad*"*, whereas in American English the converse is the case. Collins Dictionary (1979) gives "granddad" and doesn't include "grandad", and this is why "granddad" is the preferred spelling of the author.]

Memory 4, page 142 ...incense.

This was a fragrant, but strongly smelling perfume used in Catholic church services. It was also used in some Church of England services. I can remember seeing a special receptacle being swung backwards and forwards in order to release the scent into the air.

Memory 5, page 143 ...Mayday messages.

This comes from the French phrase 'm'aidez,' meaning 'help me!' It was introduced in the 20th Century to provide a distress signal to be used by ships and planes in the event of an emergency.

Memory 5, page 143 ...beef...

This is a slang expression meaning 'to complain.'

Memory 6, page 144 ...nine-hole golf course.

This was half the size of a normal course, which contained eighteen holes. Golfers started at tee number one, played their ball along the fairway while trying to avoid the bunkers full of sand, and then putted the ball along the 'green' and into the hole. They then went to tee number two and repeated the process. This was not as simple as it sounds!

Memory 6, page 144 ...practice...

English spelling, unlike that of the USA, marks the difference between the verb 'to practise' and the noun 'practice.'

Memory 7, page 146 ... Intelligence tests... Scholarship papers...

I believe that I had to reach a high standard in these examinations in order to attend a grammar school. I found them interesting and rather like a collection of puzzles.

Memory 9, page 150 ...Sir James Barrie (1860-1937)

He was a Scottish novelist and playwright, and Peter Pan (1904) was his most popular work.

Memory 10, page 152 ...cutaway parts of a picture...

Sometimes an artist will portray a solid object which appears to have part of its surface cut away so that its interior is visible. This is especially useful in non-fiction books providing technical or medical information.

Memory 12, page 156 ...dyed...

This is the past tense of the verb 'to dye,' which should not be confused with the verb 'to die.' They are called homophones because they sound the same. There are over 500 English words which can be classified as Homophones. (Terrell and Meadows: A List of English Homophones; *The Quarterly Journal of Experimental Psychology*, 1985, 37A, 627-631.)

Memory 12, page 157 ...there were also an apple, an orange...

The verb 'were' is plural because its Predicate is plural: it consists of a list of objects.

Memory 13, page 158 ...a coward.

A white feather was given to someone who was thought to be a coward. The derivation of this probably comes from fighting cockerels never having white feathers which are seen only on cross breeds. [*Editor's note.*]

Postscript, page 191 ...prefab...

This word is explained on *Notes* page 208 under the heading *Memory 1*, page 92.

Punctuation Exercises

Chapter 1, Memory 10, page 22

opposite the school on the other side of friern barnet lane was the north middlesex golf club this was a private club and the grounds extended for about half a mile 800 metres along the road and were about a quarter of a mile 400 metres wide the clubhouse was about two or three hundred yards downhill of the school and a belt of woodland extended from it northwards as far as the school and perhaps as much a hundred yards beyond this woodland which ran alongside the road was only about twenty yards 15 metres wide but it contained a great many trees and a considerable number of bushes shrubs and general undergrowth

Chapter 1, Memory 15, page 32

almost as soon as i had returned to north london and even before i had started at st. jamess school i became involved with all saints church having been a choir boy in somerset i must have shown interest in continuing to sing in church because my mothers diary has an entry for Sunday 27th may 1945 bernard starts in choir at all saints this church was situated just over half a mile one kilometre up the hill from our block of flats it was part of the church of england and the sunday morning service took place at 10.30 am

Chapter 1, Memory 17, page 36

another activity which commenced soon after my return from somerset was that i joined the cubs this organisation was an off shoot of the boy scouts which had been founded by baden-powell in 1908 he was an army officer who played an important part in the defence of mafeking 1899-1900 during the boer war in a africa he believed that reconnaissance was important in warfare and wrote two books about the subject reconnaissance and scouting 1890 and aids to scouting 1899 the purpose of his scouts association was to help boys to develop good characters and a wide variety of skills such as cooking camping tying knots handling small boats and so on eventually over sixty different badges became available for sewing on to a scouts shirt sleeve in order to show his various skills

Chapter 1, Memory 18, page 38
why did i enjoy going to the wolf cubs there were several reasons firstly we often played boisterous games which enabled us to get rid of some of our youthful energy british bulldog was one of them it involved a few boys bulldogs forming a line across the room presumably reminiscent of the traditional british thin red line the other boys had to run from one end of the scout hut to the other which meant forcing their way through the line this of course involved a certain amount of wrestling if a boy was prevented from breaking through the line he joined the bull dogs the game ended when all the boys had been captured and so had joined the line

Chapter 2, Memory 3, page 52
in 1945 my father owned an ariel motor bike which he called freddie on saturday 16th june my mother wrote in her diary bernard and charles went to malden on motor bike i was about eight and a half years old and this was probably the first time that i went for any great distance on the pillion of my fathers bike our destination wasnt the essex town of maldon but new malden which is situated within the greater london area just to the south of wandsworth and wimbledon and i believe that we used the north circular road as part of our route our purpose was to visit a model rail way track

Chapter 2, Memory 4, page 54

I dont know whether or not my father had begun to make his own locomotive before our visit to new malden in june 1945 but i doubt it from several references in his 1947 diary i believe that he must have been using his own lathe in 1946 on sunday 2nd february 1947 after it had snowed heavily he wrote in his diary broke off using lathe to make a sledge for bernard on saturday 15th february 1947 he wrote dug out loco and prepared for steam test this implies that he had already made the locomotive which would have been a time consuming process over a period of several months

Chapter 2, Memory 5, page 56

my father kept his motor bike in one of the garages which lay behind the flats two weeks after dad and i had visited the model railway club at new malden my mother noted in her diary on sunday 1st july 1945 charles and bernard went to pitsea on freddie petrol had been rationed during the war but i imagine that the restrictions had begun to be eased by the summer of 1945 although petrol rationing didnt end until saturday 27th may 1950 be that as it may that sunday in july was the first of a score of motor bike trips to my fathers relatives in essex over the next ten years although from 1950 until 1955 we travelled by motor bike and side car if she were with us my mother would sit in the side car and i would still need to sit on the pillion

Chapter 2, Memory 8, page 62

as well as going to pitsea on the occasional sunday afternoon i also enjoyed several holidays there i went for a week or so every easter from 1946-1950 and also spent a week or two there in the summer holidays of 1946 1948 and 1950 i would sleep in the bed room at the end of the lounge but i was able to spend the day doing more or less what i liked some times i played with my cousin ken over at kendorern and some times with joan and carol who were uncle daves daughters on at least once occasion cousin pam toms daughter joined joan carol and me we explored the wood land at the end of the concrete path but we never reached the far end which presumably reached rectory road

Chapter 2, Memory 9, page 66

southend lies on the left bank of the river thames about thirty five or forty miles to the east of london its a popular sea side resort for londoners especially those in the east end of london and is famous for its pier which is over a mile long when i first visited it there was a small train with open air carriages which ran from the shore out to the end of the pier some people liked to walk to the end of the pier and take the train back there were four possible permutations of getting to the end of the pier and returning but all of them involved coming in to contact with the sea breezes the allegedly healthy ozone

Chapter 2, Memory 17, page 82

i began to go to the swings when i was quite young this was a general term for various pieces of apparatus found in some public parks which were also known as recreation grounds there were swings at a recreation ground in oakleigh road only a few hundred yards east of our flats and some more swings at friary park which was situated in friern barnet lane just south east of the north middlesex gold course at each site there were swings a roundabout a slide a rocking horse a see saw and a climbing frame

Chapter 2, Memory 2, page 88

another activity which was very beneficial to me was that i learned to swim while at junior school on thursday 10th october 1946 my mothers diary records bernard swimming and cubs as usual school swimming lessons probably commenced for me in the previous september when i was just under ten years old we used to be taken by coach to bowes road swimming pool which is now called arnos swimming pool and lies only a couple of hundred yards east of arnos grove underground station we went in to a changing room through a door on the right of the entrance changed in to our swimming trunks and then went through a door at the far end of the room here we gathered at the pool side to be told what to do

Chapter 3, Memory 1, page 92

i began to play football at st jamess as part of the school curriculum and this continued until i left grammar school at the age of eighteen once a week we used to change in to our football kit in our class room and then walk around to the playing field behind the school our kit included proper foot ball boots and i believe that we only played foot ball in this way during my two years with miss leroy i enjoyed playing foot ball and some times took my boots with me to play with a few other boys in bethune park which lay only a few hundred yards down the hill from our flat i some times played with two of my class mates arthur jewell lived in russell road not very far from john browne and richard messer lived in one of the prefabs next to bethune park

Chapter 3, Memory 2, page 94

on saturday 18th january 1947 i went to join friern barnet library which was about three quarters of a mile away one and a half kilometres from our flat i had to bring a form home for my parents to sign after which i received two cardboard tickets with my name and address on them it became my custom to walk down oakleigh road past the allotment gardens and then along a road which led down to bethune park through the prefabs i walked along a path through bethune park along bethune avenue and crescent road up glenthorne road and then along friern barnet road to the library some times i would ride my bike along the same route and occasionally i would borrow a book for my mother or father as well as for myself

Chapter 3, Memory 5, page 100

after my parents married in december 1935 they moved in to a modern block of flats in the spring of 1936 this was hastings house in west ealing at some time after i was born we moved to greenford probably because this residence was only a mile or two from the ozaphone factory in perivale presumably situated on western way according to my fathers cv he went to work in the aid aeronautical inspection directorate as an examiner from 1938-1941 and then as a senior examiner from 1941-1943

Chapter 3, Memory 7, page 104

a year after the war had ended my father was transferred to a department in leicester he worked there from monday 28th october 1946 until friday 15th july 1949 at which time he returned to london fortunately for me my parents decided not to move northwards but to remain at whetstone and so i didnt have to change schools and make new friends my father commuted between the two locations leaving for leicester on monday morning and returning home on friday evening he made the trip either by train or by motor bike he had begun to keep a diary in january 1947 and some times made a note of how long his journeys took

Chapter 3, Memory 14, page 120

during the war my mother had earned some money by book keeping which she was able to do at home she started working for a firm called barrett and bolton in february 1943 but this work came to an end on friday 5th october 1945 on 11th february 1946 she noted in her diary muriel carminati came with news of a part time job at standards but it wasnt until a year later on monday 28th april 1947 that mother started work there it was light and relatively easy engineering work although probably some what repetitive but she had to be there ready for work at 8.30 am fortunately the walk took her very little time she then worked until 1.15 pm after which she returned home for the rest of the day

Chapter 3, Memory 15, page 122

my mother benefited by working at standards not only because she was able to earn her own money rather than always relying on my father but also because she was able to meet new people two of her special friends were alice stevens and gladys wilson both of whom were married alice had a daughter called betty and i still have a couple of photographs showing mother and me alice betty and gladys at southend while on a coach trip organised by standards the five of us went on such an outing to southend at least twice my mother invited both of them to our flat from time to time and also liked to visit them at their homes gladys lived at 105 fountains crescent which was a semi detached house just off winchmore hill road

Chapter 4, Memory 8, page 148

radio was an important part of my life until i was eighteen but after that it declined in importance partly because of the influence of television when i was young however my mother and i often listened to the home service and the light programme at that time the third programme was too heavy for me because it featured classical music and i preferred lighter and more popular musical entertainment however a great deal of light classical music was used as incidental music to radio programmes and so i absorbed such music with out realising it on monday 2nd february i wrote in my diary hurried home to listen to childrens hour